MW00966168

Praise from International Business Leaders for Raise Your Cultural IQ

"*Raise Your Cultural IQ* is a reference book no traveller to the Asia-Pacific region should be without. Filled with interesting facts, it will open many a door, whether the trip is for business or pleasure."

– Robert Armstrong, President
Canadian Importers Association (Canada)

"I heartily recommend *Raise Your Cultural IQ* as a handy reference guide that will help travellers avoid the social blunders that can ruin a vacation or business trip."

– Magnus Lindberg, Export Manager
BIM Kemi AB (Sweden)

"A business trip or vacation in the Asia-Pacific region can be marred by an inadvertent slight that offends your hosts. *Raise Your Cultural IQ* is designed to prevent this from happening. It's filled with handy tips about customs and taboos of more than 20 countries. Carefully researched and well laid out, *Raise Your Cultural IQ* is a must-read publication for anyone contemplating a trip to this part of the world".

– Yaro Marcen, President
Diplomat Designe (Czech Republic)

"A sensitive traveller knows that there are customs he or she should be aware of when they visit a foreign land. *Raise Your Cultural IQ* contains page after page of handy tips for making a trip more successful. The small details make a big difference."

– Alfonso Salazar, President
Ocean Garden Products Inc. (U.S.A.)

"Business and vacation travellers will welcome *Raise Your Cultural IQ* as a comprehensive guide to how to act when in one or more of the countries in the Asia-Pacific region. It contains useful phrases, tips on gifts that please and gifts that might offend. You'll be glad you brought it along."

– George Nanovfszky, General Director
CIS Department, Ministry of Foreign Affairs (Hungary)

Increase your chances for success in international business & foreign relations

LOUISA NEDKOV

Trade Winds Publications Inc.
Toronto, Canada

To my mom

Canadian Cataloguing in Publication Data

Nedkov, Louisa 1957-

Raise your cultural IQ – Asia & the Pacific

ISBN 0-9684413-0-0

1. Business travel–Asia–Guidebooks. 2. Business travel–Australia–Guidebooks. 3. Business travel–New Zealand–Guidebooks. 4. Asia-Guidebooks. 5. Australia–Guidebooks. 6. New Zealand–Guidebooks. I. Title.

HF5389.3.A78N43 1999 915.04'429 C99-900113-2

Printed and bound in Singapore

ATTENTION: BUSINESSES & SCHOOLS

If you are unable to locate this book at your nearest retail outlet, and wish to order in bulk for business or educational use, contact:

Trade Winds Publications Inc.
740 York Mills, Road, Suite 201
Toronto, Ontario, Canada
M3B 1W7

Editor: Thomas Douglas

Design: Bruce Chalmers

Maps: Steven Stanley

Research Assistance: Alanda Theriault

TABLE OF CONTENTS

ACKNOWLEDGEMENTS

My sincere thanks to the people who either contributed material or reviewed portions of the manuscript:

Bakar Aman, Counsellor, High Commission of Malaysia (Ottawa)

Ian Wood, New Zealand High Commission (Ottawa)

B. Somasiri, High Commission for the Democratic Socialist Republic of Sri Lanka (Ottawa)

W. Thanapol, Royal Thai Embassy (Ottawa)

Fay Huang, The Consulate General of the People's Republic of China (Toronto)

Nina Abramova, WTC Moscow (Russia)

Indo-Arab Chamber of Commerce Mumbai (India)

Hideki Kono (Nagano)

Merlin Peters, Merlusha (Bombay)

Kyrgyz Embassy in Moscow (Russia)

Darryl Astin, World Trade International (Australia)

World Trade Center Tokyo (Japan)

Ako Haruta, World Trade Center Osaka (Japan)

Hoa Nguyen (Kansas)

Cecilia A. Sanchez & Leikha Mulsid, WTC Metro Manila (Philippines)

World Trade Center Osaka (Japan)

Jason Wen, China World Trade Center Ltd. (Beijing, P.R.C.)

Robyn Winters, World Trade Centre Melbourne (Australia)

Lily Kam, Hong Kong Trade Development Council (Toronto)

DH Nooriyah PLW Yussof, High Commission of Brunei Darussalam

World Trade Center Sapporo (Japan)

Maki Nakamura, World Trade Center Tokyo (Japan)

Prany Sananikone, University of California, Irvine (California)

Preeya Horie, Ph.D., The National Language Research Institute (Tokyo)

Won Hyung Cho, Embassy of the Republic of Korea (Ottawa)

Marianne Ash, World Trade Centre Sydney (Australia)

Ibnu Wahyutomo, Embassy of Indonesia (Ottawa)

Thank you to Polyglot Translations for tracking down words and phrases in some of the more difficult languages.

I would also like to thank my family (mom, Rosemary, Tammy, and Brent) and my friends Juan Gabriel and Nancy for their continuing support and patience, particularly during the last month when I was glued to my computer.

And a very special thanks to my friend Ousama whose encouragement and whose gentle, yet firm nudging helped make this book a reality.

– Louisa Nedkov
Toronto, Canada
Winter, 1999

INTRODUCTION

In what culture would using your left hand for eating be considered disgusting?

When would stepping on the doorsill of a home upset the owners?

In what country would the gift of a clock be considered inappropriate?

So how well did you do answering the questions above? The answers are provided at the back of the book on pages 39, 53 and 95. Other little "test questions" can be found throughout the book (hopefully, after you have read this book, you will get a perfect score!)

In my international seminars and workshops, I always begin the program with a cultural IQ quiz. My experience has been that people are always amazed by how little they actually know about other cultures, even those who have travelled extensively and are veterans in the world of international business.

This book is designed for business people or tourists who want to reduce miscommunications and increase his or her success, in business and personal relationships, overseas. I hope this information will assist in making you feel more confident and comfortable when you attend that first formal Chinese banquet (the rules of chopstick etiquette have been provided) or go to that first meeting with your Asian colleagues (Do I bow here or shake hands?).

I have also included a section at the back of the book, which gives a very brief outline of the major Asian religions. To truly understand Asian culture, it is necessary to have at least a basic understanding of the tenets of these religions. They are key to understanding Asian beliefs, values, and even daily activities.

Each chapter in this book focuses on a different country. Along with general information about the land and its people, practical advice is provided on introductions, what to wear, how and when to eat, the do's and taboos of gift giving, topics to avoid in dinner conversation, and gestures which could cause serious offence. I have also provided some basic phrases in the most predominant language for each country. I have found, through experience, that most natives appreciate the effort a visitor takes to speak even a few simple words in their language. Even if you completely mispronounce the vocabulary (in some of the more difficult tonal languages, such as Chinese, this is inevitable), your effort surely will be welcomed.

At the end of each country section, where applicable, I have included the addresses of World Trade Centres (WTC). Because of my work with WTCs over the past 18 years, I have a particular affinity, as well as an understanding, about the kind of assistance they can provide the business person. There are, of course, many other excellent local organizations, including your own country's embassy or consulate, where you can obtain assistance.

One of the problems with producing a book of this nature is the potential to create a stereotype of a particular culture. Please remember that this book is only meant to be a guideline for how to behave more respectfully in other countries. People are individuals and there are always exceptions to the rule. For example, the Thai people have been described as easy-going, fun-loving, and hospitable. Somewhere there is probably a serious, up-tight, not-so-generous Thai (although I personally have never met one).

I have had the great pleasure of travelling extensively throughout the Pacific Rim and have found the hospitality in this part of the world truly exceptional. If you have not had the opportunity to visit the Asia/Pacific region, I hope this book inspires you to consider making your next trip there. If you are about to embark on your first trip, may this book provide you with enough of the "basics" to make it less stressful and more successful. And for those of you who are an experienced in the world of international travel and business, I am confident you will still find many tasty new morsels of knowledge within these pages.

ASIA AND THE PACIFIC

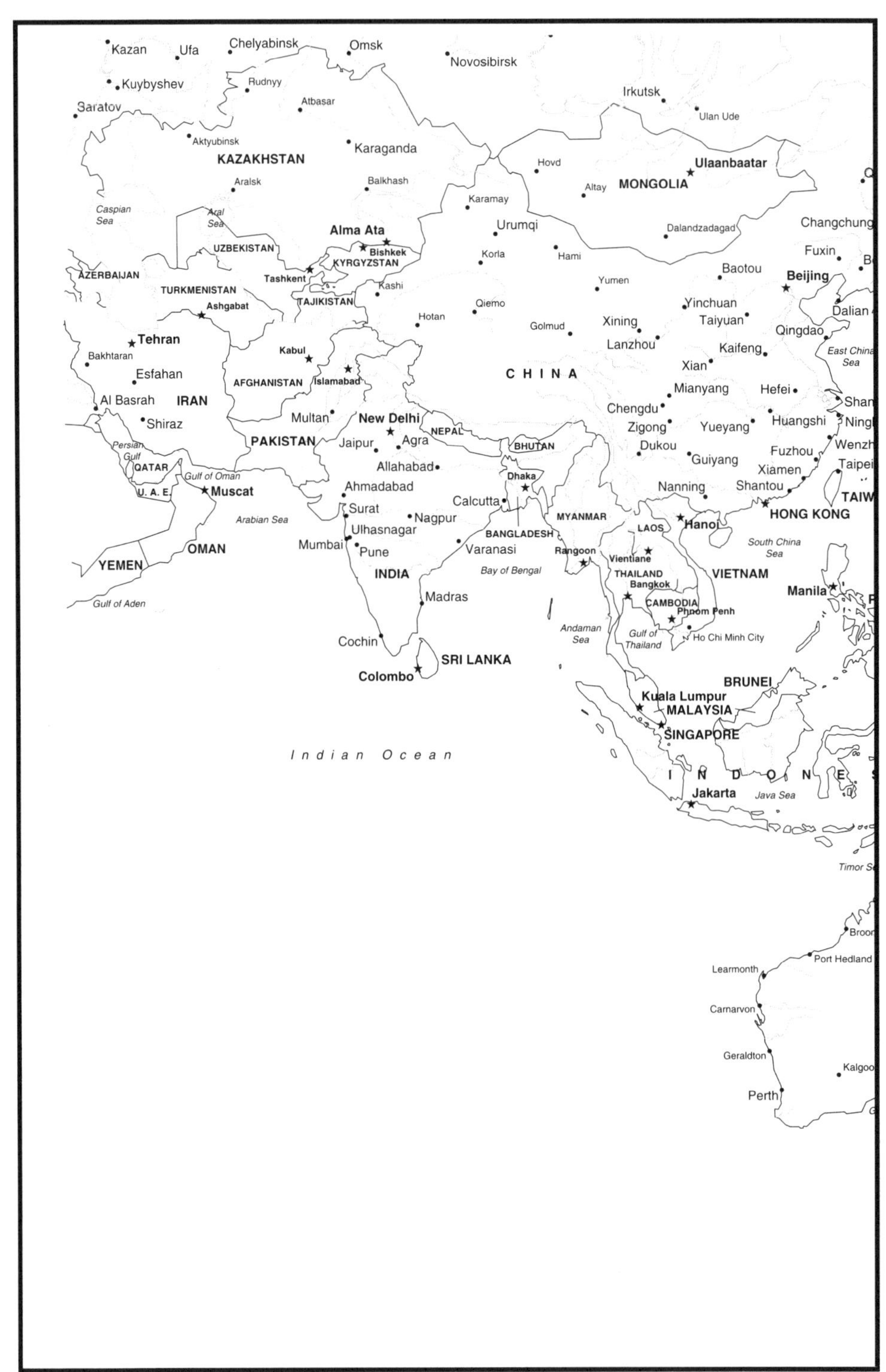

ASIA AND THE PACIFIC

AUSTRALIA

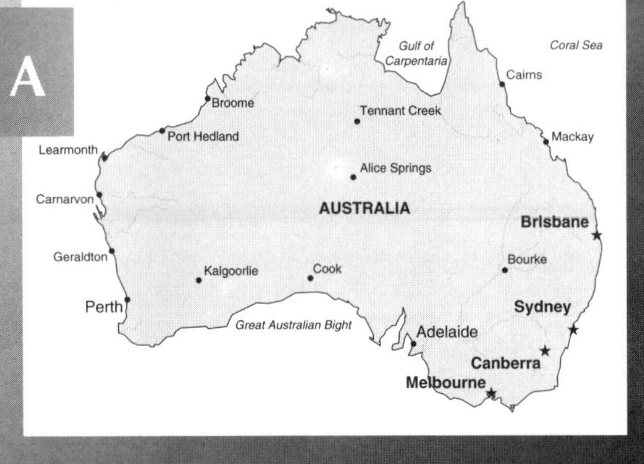

THE COUNTRY

Population

- 18.6 million and growing slowly at a rate of 1.3% per year.
- Over 90% of the population lives within fifty miles of the coast in one of the seven urban centres.

Capital

- Canberra (270,000)

Major Cities

- Sydney (4.1 million)
- Melbourne (3.2 million)
- Brisbane (1.5 million)
- Perth (1.3 million)
- Adelaide (1.1 million)

Government

- Parliamentary state

Climate

- Australia's landmass of nearly 7.7 million km2 is the flattest and (after Antarctica) driest of continents, yet has extremes of climate and topography.
- There are rainforests and vast plains in the north, snowfields in the southeast, desert in the centre and fertile croplands in the east, south and southwest.
- About a third of the country lies in the tropics.
- Summer is December through February (although an "Indian summer" climate has been experienced through to beginning/middle of April in the last few years).
- Winter is June through August.
- Climates range from wet and humid tropical conditions in the far north, through warm and temperate on the central east and west coasts, to cooler conditions in the southern coasts and Tasmania.
- It seldom snows in or near the large centres of population.

Electricity

- 220 volts
- Electrical outlets require plugs with two or three flat angled prongs.

Sports

- Tennis, sailing, golf, various water sports, Australian rules football, Ruby Union football, Rugby League football, cricket, soccer, hockey and horseracing.

Currency

- Australian dollar (A$)

BUSINESS HOURS

Business & Government Offices

- Monday through Friday: 9:00 a.m. to 5:00 p.m.
- Lunch is usually taken at noon for one half to one hour.
- Saturdays: 9:00 a.m. to 12:00 noon

Banks

- Bank times can vary, depending upon the bank.
- Monday to Friday: 9:00 a.m. to 4:00 p.m. or 5:00 p.m.
- Some banks open Saturday mornings: 9:00 a.m. to 12:00 noon.

Department Stores

- Monday through Friday: 8:30 a.m. to 5:30 p.m.
- One evening a week, usually Thursdays, shops stay open until 9:00 p.m.
- In large cities, may remain open late on the weekends.
- Some shops open on Sundays

HOLIDAYS & FESTIVALS

New Year's Day....................................January 1
Australia Day........ Last Monday of January*
Good Friday, Easter.................March or April**
Anzac Day..April 25
Queen's Birthday........Second Monday in June
Melbourne Cup Day............................November***
Christmas Day.................................December 25
Boxing Day.......................................December 26

*(Holiday now has to be taken on January 26, no matter what day it falls upon)
**four days including the following Monday
***Holiday only in Melbourne

THE PEOPLE

Ethnic Groups

- 1/3 of Australia's population is younger than 20 years of age.
- 95% of the population are Caucasian; 60% of these have Anglo-Celtic heritage.
- Because of the large immigrant population, Australia is truly a multicultural nation: Cambodian, Dutch, Estonian, French, German, Greek, Italian, Latvian, Lithuanian, Polish, Polynesian, Vietnamese, Yugoslavian, and a host of other Asian and Latin nationalities make up this country's diverse ethnic mix.
- 1.5% of the population are Aborigines that have their own distinct culture.

Language

- Australia's official language is English, by common usage rather than law.
- Australian English does not differ significantly from other forms of English, although some colloquial and slang expressions are unique.
- Chinese is the second most frequently spoken language.
- Aborigines have 50 languages (reduced from 250).

Religion

- 76% are Christian, split evenly between Roman Catholics and Protestants.
- Remaining 24% constitute other denominations.
- Generally, religion does not play a major role in day-to-day life.

CONDUCTING BUSINESS

Meeting & Greeting

- Australians are friendly, informal and relaxed. Although Australians will address visitors by their first names quite quickly, visitors should wait to be invited to do the same.
- A firm and warm handshake is extended by business people at introductions, as well as at the beginning and completion of meetings.
- Business cards should be presented at meetings.
- It is important to be relaxed, friendly and modest.
- Do not focus on trying to make a good impression, as Australians are not easily impressed. Anything suggesting pretension of status-consciousness will be viewed unfavourably.
- Prior to beginning a meeting, it is important to have brief casual discussions to establish rapport.
- Give sufficient notice when making appointments, at least one week in advance. The day before, or on the day of the meeting, call to confirm.
- Because of their egalitarian philosophy, it is generally not difficult to obtain appointments with any Australian regardless of how high their position.

Forms of Address

- Upon initial greetings, apply traditional English forms of address: Mr., Mrs., Miss, and Ms.
- There is a growing preference for women to use Ms instead of Mrs. or Miss.
- The general term "Sir" is considered respectful and appropriate in formal situations.
- Although Aborigines are addressed in the same manner as other Australians, increasingly there is a trend towards being referred to as a member of a clan rather than a tribe. The correct forms of address are currently being amended.

ENTERTAINING

- Business lunches and dinners are common.
- Lunches are usually reserved for conducting business, whereas dinners are used for socializing.

DINING ETIQUETTE

- Do not discuss business during meals or at social occasions.
- *Dinner*, the main meal of the day, is eaten in the evening. Smaller evening meals may be referred to as tea and are served between 6:00 p.m. and 7:00 p.m.
- *Afternoon tea* is served around 4:00 p.m.
- *Supper* refers to a late evening snack.
- Beer is the national drink.
- The Continental style of eating is preferred, although other dining styles are tolerated.
- Move the spoon away from you when eating soup.
- Salads are sometimes served with the main course (in place of hot vegetables or as an accompaniment).
- To indicate you are finished, place your utensils placed parallel on the plate.
- Use a wave of the hand to gain a waiter's attention at a restaurant.
- In pubs, it is important that each person pay for a round of drinks. Missing your opportunity to *Shout for a round* will definitely leave a bad impression.
- In private homes, you will normally receive a plate of food, rather than helping yourself to various dishes.

PUNCTUALITY

- Punctuality is important for meetings.
- Do not make unannounced visits. It is important to call in advance.

USEFUL PHRASES

- The following is a list of words in Australian English and their meanings in North American English:

Mate
Friend, pal or buddy

Fair go
A fair, reasonable chance

Arvo
Afternoon

No worries
No problem

Tele
Television

Barbie
Barbecue

Ta
Thank you

Tall poppy
High achiever

Tucker
Food

Fair dinkum
"Honest, it's the truth!"

Bickies
Money

Bathers
Swimming costume

Crust
Your livelihood

Globe
Lightbulb

Ripper
Terrific!

Bloody Oath
On my oath

She'll be right
Don't worry

Ya
You

VALUES AND SOCIAL CONVENTIONS

- Australians are adverse to class distinctions and resent anyone who acts in a pretentious manner or "puts on airs".
- Modesty is important. Downplay your knowledge and importance. Do not flaunt your educational background.
- Australians are very direct.
- Australians are reluctant to praise. When commending anyone, it will be done in a joking or sardonic manner.
- Private life and leisure are very important to Australians.
- Australians are "laid back" and easygoing.
- The pace of life is slower compared to North America.

BODY LANGUAGE

- The "thumbs up" gesture is considered offensive if motioned vertically upwards. If held, the gesture can mean "she'll be right" or "good on ya".
- When yawning, it is important to cover your mouth and excuse yourself. It is considered a sign of boredom.
- Winking at women is considered inappropriate.
- Forming a "V" with your index and middle finger, palm facing in, is considered vulgar.
- Pointing with your index finger is impolite. Use an open hand.
- Avoid sniffing repeatedly if you have a cold. Politely excuse yourself to blow your nose in private.
- Due to sexual harassment laws, people should avoid being too physical.

CONVERSATION

- Australians are world famous for their love of all sport, but they are also enthusiastic supporters of the arts and communications industries.
- Politics and religion are taken seriously. Anticipate strong opinions.
- Australians enjoy controversy and express respect by challenging others.
- Avoid using North American slang as Australians may find some expressions offensive.
- Australians enjoy and appreciate informal and spontaneous humour.

TIPPING

- Although tipping is not required, it is becoming increasingly common in restaurants due to the influx of tourists.
- A small tip is appreciated for good service.

DRESS & APPEARANCE

- Fashion follows North American styles with a slant towards informality.
- Business clothing tends to be conservative, usually a dark suit and tie for men.
- Tailored suits, skirts, blouses and dresses for women.

GIFTS

- Gifts are not generally exchanged in a business environment.
- A gift of flowers, wine, chocolates or crafts from your native country are appreciated, but not necessary, when invited to a home for dinner.

FOR WOMEN

- Women comprise 38% of the workforce.
- Australia does not present any substantial barriers to the foreign women wanting to do business here.

USEFUL ADDRESSES

World Trade Center Melbourne
Level 4
Melbourne Exhibition and Convention Centre
2 Clarendon Street
Southbank 3205, Australia
Fax: (61 3) 92538852
Tel: (61 3) 92056400
Email: pgillesp@mcec.com.au

World Trade Centre Sydney
Level 12, 83 Clarence Street
Sydney, NSW 2000
Australia
Fax: (61 2) 9350 8199
Tel: (61 2) 9350 8100
Email: wtc@giga.net.au

BANGLADESH

THE COUNTRY

Population
- 123 million
- One of the most densely populated countries in the world.
- One of the world's poorest countries.

Capital
- Dhaka (8.5 million)

Major Cities
- Chittagong (2.5 million)
- Khulna (1 million)

Government
- Democracy divided into four regions.
- Central government is led by a prime minister.
- The president is the head of state.

Climate
- Bangladesh has a tropical climate with three distinct seasons.
- Winter (October to March) is cool and mild.
- Summer (March to June) is hot and humid.
- The monsoon season (June to October) brings most of Bangladesh's yearly rain.
- Floods, tidal waves, and cyclones are common.
- The average annual temperatures range between 23C (73F) and 30C (86F).
- Summer temperatures may reach as high as 39C (102F).

Electricity
- 220 volts
- Electrical outlets require plugs with either two thin, round pins or three round prongs.

Sports
- Soccer, field hockey, cricket, table tennis, and badminton are popular.

Currency
- The *taka.*

BUSINESS HOURS

Business Offices
- Saturday to Thursday:
  8:00 a.m. to 5:00 p.m.

Government Offices
- Saturday to Thursday:
  7:30 a.m. or 8:00 a.m. to
  2:00 p.m. or 2:30 p.m.

Banks
- Saturday to Wednesday:
  9:00 a.m. to 11:30 a.m.
- Thursday: 9:00 a.m. to 11:00 a.m.

Stores
- Saturday to Thursday:
  10:00 a.m. to 8:30 p.m.
- Friday is a holiday for offices, banks, and most stores.

HOLIDAYS & FESTIVALS

Shabe-e-Barat	January*
National Mourning (Martyrs) Day	February 21
Ramadan	*
Eid-ul-Fitr	*
Independence Day	March 26
Bengali New Year	April 15
Buddha Purnima	May*
Eid-ul-Azha	May/June*
Eid-e-Miladunnabi (the Prophet Muhammad's Birthday)	September*
Durga Puja	October*
Diwali	October/November*
National Solidarity Day	November 7
Victory Day	December 16
Christmas Day	December 25

*date varies

THE PEOPLE

Ethnic Groups

- 98% Bengali
- 1% Bihari tribesmen
- 1% Garo, Khasi, Santal
- 85% of the population live in the rural areas.
- The Bangladeshis have an Indo-European heritage, but it has also been touched by the Burmese, Tibetan, Arab Muslim, Persian, Turk, Afghan and Mughal cultures.

Language

- The official language is Bangla.
- Several distinctive dialects exist.
- Most dialects are quite soft and musical in nature.
- Most professionals and students speak English.
- The Biharis speak Urdu (the official language of Pakistan).
- The small ethnic groups which live along the borders speak their own languages.

Religion

- 86% of the population are Muslim (primarily Sunni Muslim).
- Bangladesh is home to the second largest Muslim population in the world.
- 13% of the population are Hindu.
- 1% practice Buddhism.
- There is a small Christian minority.

CONDUCTING BUSINESS

Meeting & Greeting

- Men commonly greet one another with a handshake.
- It is advisable to wait for a Bangladeshi woman to offer her hand. The most appropriate greeting is often a simple nod and a smile.
- Many Bangaldeshi will greet one another using the traditional Indian *namaste*. Both hands are placed together, as in prayer, at chest level. This is accompanied by a slight bowing of the head.
- The common verbal greeting between Muslim Bangladeshis is *Assalaamualaikum* (Peace be upon you). The response is *Waalaikum assalaam* (And peace be upon you). This is often accompanied by a gesture similar to a salute, whereby the right hand is raised to the forehead, with a curved palm.
- A common verbal greeting between Hindus is *Adab* (Hello). When departing, a Hindu may say *Khoda hafiz* (May God be with you).
- A common phrase which is used by all groups when departing, is *Ashi* (so long).
- Before the meeting begins, business cards are exchanged.
- A few minutes of casual conversation should precede formal business discussions.

Forms of Address

- There are no hard and fast rules on the order of names.
- Some Muslims use family names, whereas others may not.
- Among the business community, the correct way to address a Muslim Bangladeshi is with the English courtesy titles (Mr., Mrs., or Miss) followed by the family name.
- Between Bangladeshis, the terms "sister" and "brother" are often used for friends and colleagues, in addition to family members.
- The Bangladeshi pay heed to the age of a person. If someone is older, he or she may be addressed by name plus a family-related suffix. People of or near the same age address each other by name only.
- A Hindu name is either preceded by *Sri* (for men) or *Srimati* (for married women) or followed by *Babu* (for men). An unmarried woman is addressed as *Kumari*, followed by her last name.
- Hindus often use *Sahib* to address professional people (i.e. Doctor *Sahib*).

ENTERTAINING

- Business entertaining is common and considered an opportunity to further develop relationships.
- Business dinners are more common than lunches. Business breakfasts are rare.
- It is common to be invited to a Bangladeshi's home for dinner, once a relationship has been established.
- There is very little conversation during the course of the meal.
- In traditional Muslim homes, the hostess may not join the guests for dinner. Muslim women eat separately from men.
- Shoes should be removed before entering a home.

DINING ETIQUETTE

- Most Bangladeshis do not eat pork or drink alcohol (due to the Islamic influence).
- Food is eaten using the right hand only.
- Utensils are not used, except in the case of sweets where a spoon may be used.
- Any bones, or other food debris, should be placed on "bone plates", separate from the main meal.

PUNCTUALITY

- Although the Bangladeshis have a relaxed attitude towards time, punctuality is appreciated from foreign business visitors.
- Foreign visitors should be punctual for social occasions. Bangladeshis will avoid being the first or the last to arrive.

USEFUL PHRASES

Yes
(han)

No
(naa)

Hello
(hallo)

How are you?
(Kamon achhen)

Please
(Doya kore amake din)

Thank you
(Dhon-no-bad)

You're welcome
(Apo-nake swa-gotom)

Good morning
(Shupro-baht)

Good afternoon
(Shuvo-din)

Good evening
(Shuvo sondha)

Excuse me
(Khoma dorben)

No, I do not understand
(Na, ami bhuste parini)

Good-bye
(Bidai)

Cheers
Rarely used

VALUES AND SOCIAL CONVENTIONS

- 85% of the workforce are employed in agriculture-related industries.
- The literacy rate is 48% for men and 24% for women.
- Family plays a central role in Bangaldeshi society.
- The needs of the family always take precedent over the individual.
- The Bangladeshi are class conscious.
- Bangladeshis are not comfortable saying an outright "no". Questions requiring discussion, rather than yes/no answers are recommended.
- Bangladeshis do not like to be the bearer of bad or negative news. If there is a problem, it will either be ignored or hidden.
- It is not customary for a Bangladeshi to say "thank you", except in formal situations. The Bangladeshi instead prefer to reciprocate the favour.
- Bangladeshis drive on the left side of the road.

BODY LANGUAGE

- It is polite for non-practicing Muslims to avoid eating, drinking, or smoking in front of Muslims during *Ramazan* (*Ramadan*, the month of fasting).
- Shoes must be removed before entering mosques and temples.
- Direct eye contact during a conversation indicates sincerity.
- Do not photograph people, particularly women, without asking their permission.
- The North American "okay" gesture (thumb and index finger touching to form a circle) is considered obscene.
- It is considered impolite to point at a person using the bottom of the shoe or foot.
- Do not touch books or other reading materials using your foot.
- It is considered impolite to cross your legs or smoke in front of an older person.
- Do not use the "thumbs up" gesture. It is considered a sign of rejection.
- Do not point using the index finger. The polite way is to point using the chin.
- It is considered impolite to beckon adults.

- The polite way to beckon is to extend the hand out, palm down and all fingers waving together.
- The left hand is reserved for bodily hygiene and therefore considered "unclean". Eat and touch other people using the right hand only. Pass objects to others using the right hand or both hands.

CONVERSATION

- Good topics of conversation include: sports, positive remarks about Bangladesh, your travels, and general questions about someone's family and children. Unless you know an individual well, it is not acceptable to ask about his wife.

TIPPING

- Tipping is common.
- In better restaurants and hotels: 10% of the bill is appropriate (if a service charge has not already been included).
- Taxis: round up to the nearest *taka.*

DRESS & APPEARANCE

- Because of the warm climate, conservative, lightweight clothing is appropriate.
- For initial meetings, businessmen should wear a suit, shirt, and tie.
- A shirt, slacks and tie may be all that is required for subsequent meetings. Follow the lead of your Bangaldeshi colleagues.
- For women, suits or dresses are appropriate. Pants are acceptable and appropriate because they cover the legs.
- Women should avoid wearing short, sleeveless or revealing clothing.
- Bangladeshi men generally wear western-style clothing, particularly in the cities.
- Bangladeshi women generally wear a traditional *saree.* Women do not wear pants. Jewellery is an important part of their attire.
- Most women will cover their heads with a thin scarf called a *dupatta.*

GIFTS

- Business gifts are not required for initial meetings.
- For subsequent meetings, modestly priced gifts such as a handicraft from your home country or a pen set are suitable.
- When visiting a home, it is appropriate to bring a gift. Suitable gifts include local sweets, chocolates or something for the children.

FOR WOMEN

- Bangladesh is a male dominated society.
- Although women comprise only 7% of the workforce, some have excelled in various professions including government and business.
- Except in the upper class, women are generally considered inferior.
- *Purdah* is observed by some women. This means they are "veiled" and out of sight of all men (except family members).

BRUNEI

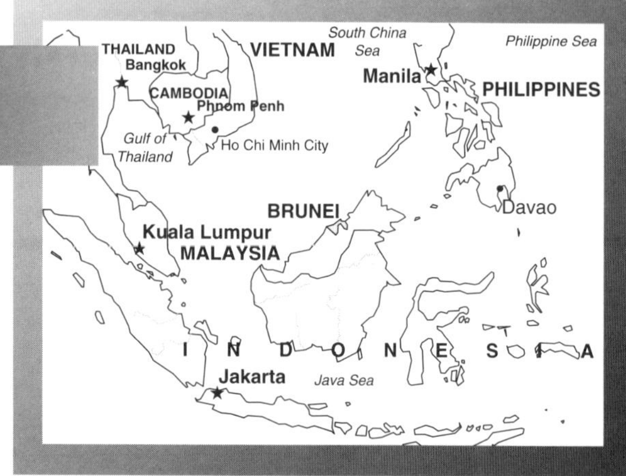

THE COUNTRY

Population
- 323,600
- 43% of the inhabitants are below the age of 20.

Capital
- Bandar Seri Begawan (187,000)

Government
- Sultanate Monarchy

Climate
- Tropical climate with high temperatures and humidy and heavy rainfall.
- No marked seasons.
- Average daily temperature ranges between 23C (73F) and 35C (95F).
- Relative humidity is high with an average fluctuation between 67% and 91% throughout the year.
- The monsoon season begins in November and ends in February.
- During the monsoon season, temperatures are lower, averaging about 28C (82F).

Electricity
- 220 - 240 volts
- Electrical outlets require plugs with either two round, thick pins, or three rectangular prongs.
- It would be wise to carry both.

Sports
- Soccer is the most popular sport.
- *Silat* (Malay martial art), *sepak takraw* (game using the feet or head to propel a rattan ball to the net), *gasing* (competiton with highly polished giant tops), badminton, sailing, windsurfing, cycling, and golf are also popular.

Currency
- The *Brunei Dollar* (B$)
- Singapore dollars widely accepted.

BUSINESS HOURS

Business Offices
- Monday to Thursday and Saturday: 7:45 a.m. to 4:30 p.m.
- Daily break from 12:15 noon to 1:30 p.m.
- Many offices are closed on Saturday afternoon as well as on Friday and Sunday.
- Brunei Shell Petroleum (primary company in the country) is closed on Saturday and Sunday.

Government Offices
- Monday to Thursday and Saturday: 7:30 a.m. or 8:00 a.m. to 4:30 p.m.
- Daily break from 12:00 noon to 1:00 p.m. or 1:30 p.m.
- Closed on Fridays and Sundays.

Banks
- Monday to Friday: 9:00 a.m. to 3:00 p.m.
- Saturday: 9:00 a.m. to 11:00 a.m.

Stores
- Monday to Saturday: 8:00 a.m. or 9:00 a.m. to 9:00 p.m.
- Many department stores are open seven days a week.
- During *Ramadan* the workday is often shortened.

HOLIDAYS & FESTIVALS

New Year's Day....................January 1
Chinese New Year..............January/February*
National Day and Israk Mekraj......February 23
Ramadan..................*
Good Friday..................March/April*
Hari Raya Aidi Fitri..................April*
Armed Forces Day..................May 31
Hari Raya Haji..................*
Muslim New Year
(First Day of Hijrah)..................July*
Birthday of His Majesty..................July 15
The Prophet's Birthday..................September*
Christmas Day..................December 25

*date varies

THE PEOPLE

Ethnic Groups

- 67% Malay
- 15% Chinese
- 6% Indigenous peoples such as Murut and Dusun
- 12% Indians, Europeans, and other ethnic groups
- Because of many cultural and linguistic differences, the Brunei Malays are quite distinct from the larger Malay populations in Malaysia and Indonesia.

Language

- The official language is Bahasa Melayu (Malay).
- English is widely understood and spoken, particularly in business.
- Chinese and Iban are spoken as well.

Religion

- 65% Muslim
- 12% Buddhist
- 9% Christian
- In the 1959 constitution, Islam was declared the state religion.
- The sultan serves as the head of the religion.
- Although religious freedom is tolerated, in the past several years Brunei has moved closer towards Islamic fundamentalism. Alcohol was banned in 1991. Stricter dress codes are enforced.

CONDUCTING BUSINESS

Meeting & Greeting

- The customary greeting is a handshake accompanied by a slight nod of the head.
- Brunei women, unless of the Christian faith, will not usually shake hands.
- Foreign business people should wait until a hand is offered.
- A Muslim man may indicate the greeting is from the heart by bringing his hand brought back to touch his chest.
- Business cards are always exchanged.
- Business cards should be presented and received using both hands.
- To show respect, the business card should be read before storing it away (preferably in a business card case, rather than a wallet).
- Business cards should have your title and department indicated.
- The first few minutes should be spent in casual conversation before commencing serious business discussions.
- A follow-up letter after a meeting is recommended.
- Introductions can help establish credibility. Take the time to establish the appropriate contacts.

Forms of Address

Malay Muslims:

- Many Malays will use their given name as their first name and their father's given name as their last name. (Example: If your name was Michael and your father's name was Tom, you would be called "Michael Tom" in Malay).
- Address people with the appropriate courtesy or professional title (Mr., Mrs., Dr.) and the surname.
- Titles are considered very important. Be sure to know a person's correct title before making an introduction.
- A woman retains her maiden name upon marriage.
- Sometimes, usually in formal situations, *bin* (son of) is used followed by the father's name.
- Similarly, a female would use *binti* (daughter of).
- The respectful prefix of *Encik* (for men) and *Cik* (for women) may be used before the person's given name.
- The titles *Haji* (for men) and *Hajjah* (for women) are given to those who have completed the pilgrimage to Mecca.
- If one's father has been to Mecca *Haji* (abbreviated to *Hj*) will follow *bin* or *binti*. This style is primarily used in very formal correspondence, but may be disregarded for oral purposes.

- The correct oral form of address for the Sultan and his wife, is Your Majesty and his second wife, Your Royal Highness. When writing, address correspondence to His/Her Majesty and Her Royal Highness respectively.
- Do not address a Bruneian by first name until invited to do so.

Chinese:

- Chinese Bruneians have three names. The first of the three names is the surname.
- Some Chinese Bruneians have adopted Western names.
- Address Chinese Bruneains with the appropriate courtesy or professional title (Mr., Mrs., Dr., etc.) and the surname.

ENTERTAINING

- Business meetings are held over lunch or dinner. Breakfast meetings are rare.
- Business is seldom discussed over a meal, as Bruneians do not consider it appropriate.
- Meals are considered an opportunity to socialize and to get to know one another.
- Although there are few Malay restaurants, many Chinese restaurants exist.
- Some entertaining is conducted at private clubs.
- Night life is almost nonexistent.
- Liquor is served only at Western hotels and some Chinese restaurants.
- An invitation to a Bruneian's home is unlikely in the early stages of business.

DINING ETIQUETTE

- Always use the right hand when eating, as the left hand is considered unclean.
- Muslim Bruneians customarily eat with their fingers rather than with utensils.
- Foreign visitors may be given Western-style utensils and it is appropriate to use them.
- When eating Chinese, chopsticks will be used.
- Chopsticks, when not in use, should be left on the chopsticks rest or on the corner of your plate. Never leave them standing in a bowl of rice as this is associated with a funeral ritual.
- When taking food from a communal dish, if utensils are unavailable, always use the reverse ends of your chopsticks. Do not use the ends which have been in your mouth.
- It is polite to accept even just a little food and drink when offered. When refusing anything offered, it is polite to touch the plate lightly with the right hand.

PUNCTUALITY

- Bruneians have a high regard for punctuality.
- It is important to call ahead and advise if you will be delayed for a meeting.

USEFUL PHRASES

Hello
Apa Khabar
(ah-pah kah-bahr)

Good-bye
Selamat tinggal
(she-lah-maht ting-gahl

Yes
Ya
(yah)

No
Tidak
(tee-dahk)

Good morning
Selamat pagi
(she-lah-maht pah-ghee)

Good afternoon
Selamat petang
(she-lah-maht pet-tahng)

Good evening
Selamat malam
(she-lah-maht mah-lahm)

Please
Minta
(min-tah)

Thank you
Terima kasih
(tree-mah kay-say)

You're welcome
Sama sama
(sah-mah sah-mah)

VALUES AND SOCIAL CONVENTIONS

- Few hotels cater to international visitors.
- Brunei has one of the highest per-capita incomes in the world.
- Citizens pay no tax and their minimum wage is the highest in the region.
- Avoid eating or drinking in the presence of Muslims during Ramadan, the month of fasting.
- Driving is on the left-hand side of the road.
- Bruneians are warm, friendly, and hospitable. People tend to smile only when they are happy.
- Bruneians are very conservative.
- The preservation of harmony is very important.
- Bruneians will not say "no" directly. Be sure to word your questions to avoid a yes/no response.
- Decision making may proceed slowly because of bureaucracy. Be patient.
- Relationships are very important to succeeding in business. Take the time to establish trust and relationships with your Bruneian colleagues.
- Islamic enforces strict legislation. It prohibits a non-Muslim to be in secluded company with a Muslim of the opposite sex. You could be prosecuted.

BODY LANGUAGE

- Do not eat or drink while walking in public. It is considered rude.
- Public displays of affection are seen to be in bad taste.
- Casual contact with members of the opposite sex will make Bruneian Muslims feel uncomfortable and should be avoided.
- Bruneians are prohibited from singing or dancing in public.
- It is considered very impolite to lean on a table or chair where someone is seated, especially if visiting an official or colleague in an office.
- It is considered overbearing to rest your feet on a table or chair.
- Do not sit on a table while speaking to a person who is seated behind it.
- When walking in front of people, especially the elderly and those senior in rank or position, it is a gesture of courtesy and respect for one to bend down slightly, as if bowing, to the side in the direction of the person that one is passing. At the same time, one of the arms should be positioned straight down along the side of your body.
- Avoid touching or patting someone's head, including children, as Bruneians consider this extremely disrespecful.
- There is no public contact between sexes in Brunei, even between husband and wife.
- For both Muslims, the left hand is reserved for personal hygiene and therefore considered unclean. Do not eat, accept gifts, pass objects, or hold cash with your left hand. When both hands are needed, it is acceptable to use both.
- The foot is also considered unclean. Avoid showing the soles of your feet (or shoes), touching anyone or moving objects with your feet.
- Bruneians generally sit on the floor, particularly for large gatherings. If seated on the floor, men normally sit cross-legged whereas women will sit with their legs tucked underneath them. It is considered rude to sit with legs stretched out particularly if someone is sitting in front.
- Shoes must always be removed before entering a mosque.
- To beckon someone, extend the arm out, hand down, and make a downward scratching motion with your fingers towards your body.

CONVERSATION

- Suitable topics include positive aspects about the country or discussions about your travels.
- Avoid discussing the wealth of the sultan and/or the country.

TIPPING

- There is a 10% service charge at hotels.
- Quality restaurants: 10% tip is appropriate.
- Taxi drivers: Generally not tipped.
- Hired drivers: 10% of the cost of the daily car rental fee is appreciated.

DRESS & APPEARANCE

- Foreign business men and women should dress conservatively.
- A suit and tie are suitable attire for men.
- Out of respect for the Muslim culture, women should dress modestly. Dresses or suits are appropriate. Avoid short skirts, sleeveless blouses or clinging fabrics.
- Many Bruneian Malay women wear a *tudong* (a traditional head covering).
- Bruneian Malay men who have completed the pilgrimage to Mecca, wear a white *songkok* (a sheet-like covering for the body).

GIFTS

- Business gifts are not expected or appropriate for first or subsequent meetings.
- Gifts are not required, but may be given, when visiting a home.
- Always give and receive gifts with both hands.
- Do not open gifts in the presence of the giver.

Muslim Bruneian

- If you wish to give a gift to the hostess, inappropriate gifts for a Muslim include alcohol, anything containing pork or gelatin from unspecified fats.
- Suitable gifts include: something from your native country, chocolates, sweets, and decorative items.

Chinese Bruneian

- Avoid giving clocks (associated with death) , knives (suggest the severing of relationships), handkerchiefs (symbolize grief) and white flowers (associated with mourning).
- Give gifts in even amounts.
- Do not wrap gifts in the colours of white, black or blue.

FOR WOMEN

- The women in Brunei play a vital role in national development.
- There are a number of Bruneian women holding high level positions in both the government and private sectors.
- Bruneian women are active in the economic sector and have their own business association "Perniaganita Brunei".

YOUR CULTURAL IQ

Q **In what countries would wrapping a gift in black paper be considered extremely inappropriate?**

A It is important to be aware of the significance of colour for the different cultures in Asia. Some colours signify good fortune whereas others are associated with bad luck. The colour black should not be used for wrapping paper as it is associated with death in virtually all Asian countries.

Q **In what country would you be fined for not flushing the toilet?**

A The Singapore government imposes heavy fines for not flushing the toilet as well as for chewing gum, littering or spitting.

CAMBODIA

THE COUNTRY

Population
- 11.4 million

Capital
- Phnom Penh (920,000)

Government
- Constitutional monarchy

Climate
- Tropical monsoon climate.
- Two major monsoon periods in Cambodia: May to October (heavy rains); November to March (light rains and winds).
- Rain usually occurs in the afternoon.
- The hottest month is April. Temperatures reach as high as 43C (110F).
- The coolest month is January. Temperatures average 27C (81F).

Electricity
- 220 volts
- Electrical outlets require plugs with either two flat parallel blades or two thin round pins.
- Power outages occur frequently.

Sports
- Soccer, table tennis, volleyball and badminton.
- Sports facilities are scarce because most facilities were destroyed by the Khmer Rouge or fell into decay during the 1980's (leisure activities were banned by Pol Pot).

Currency
- The *riel* (R).
- *Riels* are not allowed to be taken into or out of the country.
- Gold is sometimes used for larger transactions.
- U.S. dollars and the Thai *baht* are widely accepted.

BUSINESS HOURS

Business Offices
- Monday to Saturday:
  8:00 a.m. to 1:00 p.m. and
  3:00 p.m. to 6:00 p.m. or dusk

Government
- Monday to Saturday: 7:00 a.m. or 7:30 a.m. to 5:30 p.m.

Stores
- Monday to Saturday: 7:00 a.m. or 7:30 a.m. to 5:30 p.m.
- Some stores remain open longer.

HOLIDAYS & FESTIVALS

National Day (commemorates the Vietnamese overthrow of Pol Pot)......January 7
Tet (Vietnamese and Chinese New Year)......January/February*
Anniversary of Friendship Treaty between Cambodia and Vietnam......February 18
Cambodian New Year (three days)......April*
Victory Day (Revolution Day)......April 17
Visak Bauchea (birth of Buddha)......April*
May Day......May 1
Chrat Prea Angkal (ceremonial beginning of sowing season)......May*
Genocide Day (memorial for Khmer Rouge atrocities)......May 9
Anniversary of founding of Revolutionary Forces of Kampuchea......June 19
Anniversary of founding of People's Revolutionary Party of Cambodia...... June 28
Prachum Ben (offerings to spirits of ancestors)......September*
Festival of the Reversing Current (Water Festival)......October/November*
Anniversary of founding of the Front for National Reconstruction......December 2

*date varies

THE PEOPLE

Ethnic Groups

- 90% ethnic Khmer
- Remainder split between the Sino-Khmer (mixed Chinese and Khmer), Chams, and Vietnamese.
- The Chams are descents of the Champa Kingdom (eight century A.D.) which was centred in present-day Vietnam.

Language

- The official language of Cambodia is Khmer.
- Khmer is derived from an older language called *paali.*
- The closest languages to Khmer are Thai (Thailand) and Lao (Laos).
- Khmer can be a difficult and confusing language.
- Many educated Cambodians speak French. Businesspeople are using French more often.
- English is becoming more popular in the cities. Thc youngcr generation is interested in learning English.

Religion

- With the exception of the Chams, who practice Islam, the majority of Cambodians practice Thervada Buddhism.
- During the period between 1975 and 1979, the Khmer Rouge destroyed most Buddhist records, monasteries, temples and shrines. They also murdered a majority of the country's Buddhist monks.
- Buddhism was recognized as the state religion in 1989.
- Buddhist practices were restored based upon memory and a few books saved by educated survivors.
- The Buddhism practiced in rural areas has been combined with some Hindu beliefs as well as animism.
- The Hindu belief of fate has heavily influenced the lack of Cambodian motivation to improve or change their economic and social conditions.
- The government is encouraging traditional Buddhist practices.
- Cambodians believe that a man should have a monk's education for at least three months, if not several years.

CONDUCTING BUSINESS

Meeting & Greeting

- The traditional Cambodian greeting is to place hands together in a prayer position at the chest level, without touching the body. This gesture is similar to the Indian *namaste.*
- To show greater respect, the hands can be placed higher (but never higher than the level of the nose).
- This gesture is accompanied by a slight bow when greeting persons of great status and age.
- If one is carrying something, a slight bow of the head is adequate.
- One common greeting of Cambodians is *Sok sebai.*
- Cambodian men will shake hands with foreign business people.
- Cambodian women will exchange the traditional greeting.
- Foreign business people should wait until a Cambodian woman offers her hand. Some women find it embarrassing to shake hands.
- Meetings should begin with casual conversation.

Forms of Address

- In formal situations, it is appropriate to address a man by Lok (Mr.) and the family name. Women are addressed as *Lok Srey* (Mrs.) and the family name.
- It is also appropriate to address an individual by Mr. or Mrs. followed by their first name.
- To address friends, use *Mith* followed by the first name.
- A monk should be addressed as *Prek Som.*
- Royalty should be addressed as "Your Highness" or "Your Majesty".
- In informal situations, Cambodians will address an older man as *Bang.* An older woman will be addressed as *Bang Srey.*
- These terms are used to indicate degree of respect and rank.

ENTERTAINING

- Business lunches are popular for relationship building.
- Entertaining will normally take place in hotel restaurants and bars.
- Very few hotels have running water.
- Cambodians are cautious about inviting strangers into their homes, although they are in general very hospitable and friendly.
- Shoes should be removed before entering a private home.
- In traditional homes, Cambodians will sit on floor mats when eating.
- Men will sit with their legs crossed, whereas women will tuck their legs to one side.

DINING ETIQUETTE

- Cambodians will eat with their hands, chopsticks, or spoons, depending upon the type of food served and family customs.
- Guests will be offered the best place to sit and the best portion of food.
- Cambodian food has been influenced by Indian, Chinese and European cuisine.
- It is considered acceptable to clean one's teeth with a toothpick following a meal, as long as the free hand is used to cover the mouth when doing so.

PUNCTUALITY

- It is important to be punctual for business meetings.

USEFUL PHRASES

Yes
(Chaa) - for women
(Bat) - for men

No
(Tay)

Please
(som meta)

Thank you
(Som arkun)

Excuse me
(Som akphey tos

Hello
(Chumreap sur)

Good morning
(Arun Surdei)

Good afternoon
(Sayarn sursedei)

Good evening
(Sursedei)

I understand
(Knom yaal)

No, I do not understand
(Tay knom min yaal tee)

Good-bye
(Chum reap lear)

Cheers
(Som ab-arr sator)

VALUES AND SOCIAL CONVENTIONS

- *Kampuchea* is the term used by Cambodians to refer to their country.
- Buddhism has been largely responsible for shaping the social values of the Cambodian people.
- The family is extremely important.
- The needs of the group or community take precedence over the individual's.
- Group harmony is important.
- Respect is always given to elders.
- The elderly are cared for by their children.
- Cambodia is a male-dominated society.
- Household budgets, in addition to the traditional role of child rearing, are the responsibility of women.
- It is considered improper to publicly embarrass another person. "Saving face" is critical.
- Cambodians will not usually give an outright "no" response. It is considered impolite.
- Do not assume that a "yes" means an affirmative. "Yes" can be interpreted as "Yes, I understand" or "Yes, I am listening".
- Self-discipline is considered important.
- The educated and business classes were eliminated by the Khmer Rouge during its four-year rule. As a result, there are few older Cambodians in business, medicine, law, engineering or education.
- The Angkor Wat (temple) is the national symbol of Cambodia. Built in the 12th century, it is the largest religious building in the world.
- Nearly 90% of the population is employed in agriculture, food processing or forestry.
- Although not often practiced due to economics, Khmer men are permitted to marry more than one woman at a time.
- Intermarriage among ethnic groups does not generally occur.
- Running water is available in only a few hotels.

BODY LANGUAGE

- Rules governing body language come from Buddhism.
- Do not touch the head of another person, even to pat a child, as the head is considered the most sacred part of the body.
- It is considered disrespectful to stand or sit in a position which is higher than that of an older person.
- Avoid raising one's voice or showing anger as it is viewed as a lack of self-control.
- When sitting, it is important not to point your feet in the direction of the Buddha image or another person. Good eye contact, a smile, and waving of the hand are considered friendly gestures.
- Shoes must be removed when entering a pagoda (places of worship and religious education).

CONVERSATION

- Good topics of conversation include positive aspects about Cambodia or your travels.

TIPPING

- Although tipping is not expected in Cambodia, it is appreciated.
- A 10% service charge is sometimes added to a hotel or restaurant bill.

DRESS & APPEARANCE

- Conservative clothing and colours are suggested for both men and women.
- Suits and ties are appropriate for men.
- Women should wear dresses, suits, or skirts and blouses.
- Western-style clothing is fairly common, particularly in the cities.
- The traditional Cambodian clothing for men is the *sarong soet*; for women, the *sampot* and *sarong.*
- The *sarong* is a large rectangular piece of cloth that is wrapped around the hips like a skirt down to the ankles.
- Young Cambodian women may wear small, coloured hats.
- The colour white is associated with death and should not be worn.

GIFTS

- Gifts are not required for initial business meetings, unless they are with a member of the royal family.
- Suitable gifts for a royal family member are elegant handicrafts from your home country.
- For other meetings, moderately priced items with your corporate logo, fine chocolates, liquors and nice pens are appropriate. Do not give cash.
- A small gift should be given when visiting a home.
- Appropriate gifts include chocolates, sweets, liquor, or handicrafts from your home country.

FOR WOMEN

- Many small businesses and proprietorships are staffed by women.
- Women do not hold any high level positions within the government.
- Because so many men were killed during the war, there are many single-parent families and widows.
- Women who are without spouses have developed small clans for mutual aid and companionship.

CHINA

THE COUNTRY

Population

- 1.2 billion
- China is the most populous country in the world.
- 1/4 of the entire world's people live in China.

Capital

- Beijing (11.3 million)

Major Cities

- Shanghai (13.6 million)
- Tianjin (9.4 million)
- Shenyang (5.1 million)
- Guangzhou (4.5 million)

Government

- Communist party-led state

Climate

- Due to the vastness of the country, temperatures and weather conditions vary considerably. There are seven climatic zones:

North-east China:

- Cold winters with little to moderate snow or rain. Beijing has very cold winters from November to February and hot and humid summers from June to September. Intense dust storms often occur in the spring. Temperatures average between -7C (20F) and 6C (42F) in winter and between 18C (65F) and 32C (89F) in summer.

Central China:

- Experiences warm and humid summers, with occasional typhoons or tropical cyclones on the coast (in August and September). Winters are short with rain.

South China:

- This area is located partly within the tropics. It is the wettest area in the summer. Typhoons are frequently experienced.

South-west China:

- Winters are mild with little rain. Summer temperatures are moderated by the altitude.

Xizang autonomous region:

- This high plateau area is surrounded by mountains. Winters are severe with light snow and hard frost.

Xinjiang and western interior:

- Arid desert climate, with cold winters. Rainfall is well distributed throughout the entire year.

Inner Mongolia:

- This area has an extreme continental climate, with cold winters and warm summers.

Electricity

- Both the 220 volt and the 380 volt systems are used in China.
- Electrical outlets vary. Three different plugs are in use: three rectangular prongs, two thin round pins, and two flat angled blades.

Sports

- Table tennis, basketball, swimming, and soccer are popular.

Currency

- The Chinese currency is called *renminbi* – literally "the people's money" (RMB).
- The *yuan* is the unit of currency (it is all called *kuai*).
- *Renminbi* cannot be purchased outside of China.

BUSINESS HOURS

Business & Government Offices

- Monday to Friday: 8:00 a.m. to 5:00 p.m. or 6:00 p.m.
- Some offices in the larger cities have implemented five-day work weeks.
- Lunch break from 12:00 noon to 2:00 p.m.

Banks

- Monday to Saturday: 8:00 a.m. to 5:00 p.m.

Stores

- Open daily: 8:00 a.m. to 6:00 p.m. or 7:00 p.m.
- Most stores in Shanghai stay open until 10:00 p.m.
- Lunch break from 12:00 noon to 2:00 p.m.

HOLIDAYS & FESTIVALS

New Year's Day	January 1-2
Spring Festival and Chinese New Year (3 days)	Late January/early February*
International Working Women's Day	March 8
Labour Day	May 1
Youth Day	May 4
Children's Day	June 1
Anniversary of the Founding of the Communist Party of China	July 1
People's Liberation Army Day	August 1
National Day	October 1-2

*date varies

THE PEOPLE

Ethnic Groups

- The primary ethnic group is the Han Chinese (92% of the population).
- Fifty-five minorities (referred to as "the National Minorities") make up the remaining 8% of the population.
- Fifteen of these minorities include more than one million people: Mongolian, Hui, Zhuang, Uygur, Tibetan, Buyi, Korean, Miao, Yi, Dong, Manchu, Bai, Yao, Tujia, and Hani nationalities.
- 72% of the population live in rural areas.
- There are extensive differences between the ethnic groups with respect to physical features, social customs, languages, and behaviour.

Language

- 70% of the population speak standard Chinese (*Putonghua*) which is based on Mandarin. It is the national language and is taught in Chinese schools, although students may speak different languages at home.
- Other principal dialects include: *Wu* (spoken in Shanghai), *Min*, *Yue* (Cantonese) and *Kejia*.
- The minorities speak their own language or dialect.
- Cantonese is spoken primarily in the Guangdong Province and Hong Kong SAR.
- Although approximately 50,000 characters exist, less than 8,000 are commonly used. Basic literacy requires a knowledge of 1,500 to 2,000 characters.
- *Pinyin*, a Romanized alphabet, was declared the official transcription system for China in 1958.
- *Pinyin* translates Chinese characters into understandable Latin letters.
- English is spoken by many business people.

Religion

- Although the government officially encourages atheism, the Constitution does guarantee freedom of rights (within certain guidelines).
- Religion plays an important role in the life of the Chinese.
- The Chinese belief system has been influenced by three major religions: Taoism, Confucianism, and Buddhism.
- These three faiths have been richly interwoven to create one vast body of faith.
- Ancestor worship is the one underlying belief that transcends all religions.
- Confucian values have greatly influenced the habits and customs of daily Chinese life for 24 centuries.
- Religious activities and public worship are closely monitored.
- Temples, monasteries and shrines have been preserved primarily for their historical significance.
- People will often worship at home.
- Approximately 5% of the population is Christian.
- It is estimated that 2% of the population is Muslim.
- In practice, the state religion is orthodox communism.
- Central to many Chinese religious beliefs is *Feng shui* (pronounced fung shway), The words mean "wind and water". *Feng shui* has been practiced for over three thousand years in China. *Feng shui* is an entire school of environmental and cultural doctrines. *Feng shui* is based on the premise that people experience happier, healthier, more prosperous lives when their homes and work environments are harmonious. New ventures or new construction will often require the blessing of a *Feng shui* master.

CONDUCTING BUSINESS

Meeting & Greeting

- Avoid scheduling meetings during the lunch break which occurs between noon and 2:00 p.m.
- For two or three weeks during the Spring Festival and Chinese New Year (the date varies according to the lunar calendar, but occurs in late January/early February), businesses close or slow down. Foreign business visitors should avoid scheduling trips during this holiday period.
- Chinese greetings are generally quite formal.
- Because the Chinese are taught not to display emotions, they may not smile at a first greeting.
- The traditional Chinese greeting is a nod or a bow, although the handshake has become increasingly common (particularly in the cities).
- Wait for the Chinese to extend their hand before initiating a handshake.
- The handshake is usually quite soft and may linger for several seconds.
- During a greeting, the Chinese will often avoid direct eye contact. Slightly lowered eyes are considered a sign of respect. Avoid prolonged eye contact as it may be uncomfortable for the Chinese as well as perceived as being rude.
- The Chinese bow with their shoulders, not by the waist (as in the Japanese bow).
- Hands should be kept out of pockets when bowing.
- After the handshake, business cards (called name cards or *ming pian* by the Chinese) should be presented and received using both hands.
- Upon receiving a business card, be sure to take a moment to review the card (even if it is in Chinese only).
- If you are seated at a table, it is polite to place the card or cards on the table in front of you in order to refer to them.
- Do not write on a person's card while in their presence.
- Cards should be stored in a proper business card holder. Do not store a person's card in your wallet and then put it in your back pocket.
- Cards should be translated into Mandarin Chinese (preferably in gold ink – the most prestigious colour) on the reverse side.
- The most common Chinese greetings used for foreign visitors is *"Ni hao"* (Hello) or *"Ni hao ma?"* (How do you do?).
- A less formal greeting, which may be used in subsequent meetings and one that is commonly used between Chinese, is *"Chi le ma?"* (Did you eat?). The response is *"Chi le"* (Yes) or *"Mei you"* (Not yet). The question is rhetorical and not intended to actually elicit information.
- When introduced to a group (for a factory or school visit), you may be greeted with applause. The correct response is to applaud back.
- The Chinese have a high regard for rank and seniority.
- The senior members of the group should be greeted first.
- If it is a group introduction, individuals should line up according to seniority with the highest ranking and senior person at the head of the line.
- Tea will probably be served.
- The Chinese will usually begin meetings with informal conversation about the weather or your trip. This will often be followed by a brief introduction about the company as well as some historical and statistical data about the area.

Forms of Address

- In Chinese names, the family name is traditionally placed first, followed by the given name.
- Address Chinese using their professional title (Engineer, Dr., President, etc.) or government title (Mayor, Councillor, etc.) followed by their family name.
- If the title is unknown, use the appropriate courtesy title (Mr., Mrs., or Miss) and their family name.
- Never address a Chinese by his or her family name alone.
- Traditionally, Chinese wives retain their maiden name. Marital status is indicated by using Madam, Mrs., *Taitai*, or *Furen.*
- Many Chinese have taken an English first name or use their initials to ease communications with English speakers.
- It is acceptable to ask how someone wishes to be addressed, if unsure about which is the family or first name.
- Only family members or close friends use first names.
- There are only 100 widely used family names. The five most common surnames are "Chang", "Wang", "Li", "Chao", and "Liu".

ENTERTAINING

- Entertaining is a critical part of Chinese business culture.
- Business lunches have become popular, but it is likely that you will be entertained at least one evening at a dinner banquet.
- Business breakfasts are not common, but you may request one.
- The Chinese are generous hosts. Banquets consisting of 12 to 20 courses are common.
- Banquets typically begin at 6:30 p.m. or 7:00 p.m. and last for approximately two hours.
- Guests should arrive on time for banquets. Spouses are not usually included in business entertaining.
- It is expected that a visitor will host at least one dinner party before departing. This should be planned in advance prior to your arrival in China. Never outdo your hosts with the degree of expense.
- Do not discuss business at dinner unless the Chinese have initiated the conversation.
- The Chinese will rarely entertain at home. It is an honour to be a guest.
- Wait for your host to indicate that it is time for you to leave.

DINING ETIQUETTE

- Seating at a banquet is always done by title and seniority.
- The guest of honour will always be placed at the head of the room, facing the door.
- If hosting a banquet, be sure to place the highest ranking person on your right (seat with the highest honour). The second highest ranking guest should be on your left.
- Use chopsticks for eating and a porcelain spoon for soup.
- Attempt to use chopsticks. It will be appreciated by the Chinese.
- Chopsticks, when not in use, should be left on the chopsticks rest or on the table. Do not place them parallel on the top of your bowl (considered bad luck) or standing straight up in the rice (associated with a funeral ritual and synonymous with death).
- Dropping your chopsticks is considered bad luck.
- It is considered rude to tap your chopsticks on the table.
- When eating rice, bring the bowl close to your mouth.
- Do not refuse any food, as this may be considered impolite. If you don't want to eat something, simply push it to the side of your dish.
- Sauces are for dipping. Do not pour them into your rice bowl.
- If dining in a restaurant, you will be served dinner at a round table with dishes in the center on a revolving tray.
- If there is more than one set of chopsticks at your place setting, one of them is to be used for taking food from serving dishes. If a second set is unavailable, use the larger end for picking up food from the serving dishes. Never use the end you put into your mouth for picking up food from other dishes.
- Wait for the host to start eating before you begin.
- Do not place bones, seeds or other debris in your rice bowl. If a separate dish is unavailable, they should be placed on the table.
- Always leave some food on your plate when finished. (Leaving a bowl completely full is also considered rude). Because China suffered through a millennia of famine, an empty plate is considered a rebuke to your host and an indication that there had not been enough to eat.
- Toasting is popular. The host offers the first toast. *Gambei* (bottoms up) is the usual toast.
- Toasts will be made throughout the dinner.
- At formal banquets, guests should be prepared to give a short and friendly speech in response.
- It is acceptable to toast with a non-alcoholic beverage.
- If you do not want more tea, leave some in your cup.
- If you smoke, cigarettes should be offered to the others in your group.
- The serving of fruit indicates the meal has concluded.
- When a banquet has ended, the host will usually rise to leave. If this does not occur, it is polite to wait ten minutes after tea and hot towels have been distributed before leaving.

PUNCTUALITY

- It is very important to be punctual for business meetings. Arriving early indicates respect for the host.
- If you are late for a meeting, the perception may be that you cannot be trusted to be a good business partner.
- Always arrive on time for banquets. Never arrive early as it will suggest that you are hungry, and you will lose face.
- If you are hosting a banquet, arrive 15 to 30 minutes prior to the appointed time. Your guests will be punctual.

USEFUL PHRASES

Yes
Shi
(Sher)

No
Bu shi
(Boo shi)

Please
Qing
(Ching)

Thank you
Xie xie
(Syeh syeh)

You're welcome
Bu xie
(Boo syeh)

Hello
Ni hao
(Nee how)

Hello (phone)
Wei
(Way)

Good morning
Zao
(Dzow)

Good afternoon
Ni Hao or Wanan
(Nee how or Wahn-ahn)

Goodbye
Zaijian
(Dzigh-jyen)

Excuse me
Dui bu qi
(Dwayi bu chi)

VALUES AND SOCIAL CONVENTIONS

- The Chinese characters for "China" mean "the Middle Kingdom" (the center of the world).
- Establish contacts before you go. In China, it is important to have connections or *guanxi* (pronounced gwahn-shee). The Chinese spend a considerable amount of time and effort establishing and nurturing their connections. To succeed in China, it is important for foreign businesspeople to build up their own *guanxi.*
- The family, including extended family and friends, is central to Chinese life.
- Family loyalty is of the utmost importance.
- Actions of the individual reflect upon the family.
- A strict birth control program was implemented in 1972 that limits couples to only one child.
- Most Chinese are modest and humble. They are unlikely to respond to a compliment.
- In all forms of business, humility is crucial.
- Traditional social values emphasize respect for the elders and reverence for ancestors.
- Being patient, kind, faithful, soft-spoken, and not easy-to-anger are qualities revered by the Chinese.
- Loud, overly expressive behaviour is seen as offensive.
- The concept of "saving face" is very important in Chinese culture. "Face" refers to a person's pride, self-respect, family honour, and reputation. "Keeping face" means avoiding embarrassment, failure, or defeat.
- Be careful to avoid causing someone to "lose face" by insulting or criticizing them in public.
- The Chinese find it difficult to say "no". To save face or maintain harmony, the Chinese will respond with "we shall see", "maybe" or with some other indirect reply.
- Harmony must be maintained. Expect the Chinese to always say yes, although it may sometimes indicate no. "Yes" may sometimes be interpreted as "yes, I understand" or "yes, I hear you".
- Avoid using colours in presentations, as colours have symbolic meanings.
- Foreign visitors should be conscious about "numbers" when conducting business in China.
- The Chinese, like many Asians, are superstitious about numbers. The number 4 is considered unlucky in China because the word for "four" sounds like the word for "death".

- The numbers 3,0, and 8 are considered favourable numbers. Three represents life and 8 indicates prosperity.
- Setting a date for the signing of a contract or a celebration dinner should be discussed with your Chinese counterparts to ensure that the dates are considered fortuitous.

BODY LANGUAGE

- Do not pat someone on the back. A smile is preferred.
- Refrain from touching the Chinese. The Chinese tend to shun bodily contact with strangers.
- Animated facial expressions and gesturing are seen as distracting by the Chinese and should be avoided during conversation.
- To beckon someone, extend your hand with the palm down and move fingers in a scratching motion towards the body. Never use the index finger to beckon anyone.
- Whistling is considered rude.
- It is common to see people of the same sex walking hand-in-hand in public. It is regarded as a sign of friendship.
- Public affection between the sexes is discouraged.
- Placing your fingers in your mouth, for whatever reason, is seen as an unclean gesture that should be avoided.
- Maintaining good posture is important.
- Feet should not be used to point at something or to move objects.
- Never put your feet on a desk or chair.
- Do not point using the index finger. The Chinese point with an open hand.
- The Chinese generally stand in closer proximity to one another than do North Americans or Europeans.
- A common Chinese gesture to indicate that a proposal is surprising or difficult is sucking in air quickly and audibly through their lips and teeth. It is best to try to modify your request if this reaction is received.
- In some parts of China, it is common to see people spit on the sidewalk or street. Although it is not considered rude, to try to eliminate this behaviour the government has imposed fines.
- The Chinese, if they are nervous or embarrassed, may attempt to disguise their emotions by smiling or laughing.
- The Chinese are not accustomed to lining up (queuing).

CONVERSATION

- Good topics of conversation include the weather, Chinese sites, art, calligraphy, your travels, the excellent cuisine, and inquiries about the health of your colleague's family.
- Avoid discussing politics, the government, Taiwan and human rights issues.
- The Chinese are proud of their history and achievements. Avoid negative comments about the country.

TIPPING

- Tipping in restaurants was traditionally seen as insulting – something a superior does for an inferior – but with economic change it has become accepted.
- Although tipping is not expected from Chinese locals, it is expected from foreigners.
- Restaurants: Extra change is adequate, unless hosting a banquet (a gratuity should be provided for exceptional service).
- Taxis: Extra change, unless the driver assists with the luggage.
- Toilet attendants, porters, and coat-check attendants: Small change.
- Drivers and maids: A small tip is appropriate.

DRESS & APPEARANCE

- Men and women should dress conservatively. Avoid appearing flamboyant.
- Colours and styles should be kept simple, subtle and modest.
- Formal attire for men is a suit and tie.
- Women should avoid wearing provocative styles, excessive amounts of jewellery and flashy prints.
- Pantsuits are acceptable and considered suitable for even formal occasions.
- For casual wear, jeans are acceptable for both men and women.
- Shorts should be worn for recreational sports and exercising only.

GIFTS

- Be prepared to give a gift of modest value at the initial meeting.
- Gifts of value should be presented upon the conclusion of a business transaction.
- If the gift is to be given to the group, it should be presented to the leader of the delegation.
- Otherwise gifts should be presented to "each member" of the group, in the order that they were introduced.
- Gifts of value should not be given to specific individuals, as this may result in embarrassment or problems for the recipient.
- Gifts should be given and received using both hands.
- In order not to appear greedy, Chinese will normally decline a gift several times before accepting. It is important to insist until they accept the gift.
- Similarly, you should decline several times before taking a gift.
- The gift is not opened in the presence of the giver.
- Gifts should be simply wrapped.
- Avoid the colours white,blue or black for wrapping paper (associated with death).
- Because the colour red is very auspicious, it is an ideal colour to use for wrapping gifts.
- Other good colour choices for wrapping paper are pink and yellow as they are associated with prosperity and happiness.
- Do not wrap gifts prior to your arrival in China, as they may be opened by customs.
- Do not use red ink for writing on a note or card, however, as it implies the severing of a relationship.
- Moderately priced gifts include: pens, books, imported liquor, chocolates, and company logo gifts.
- If invited to a home, appropriate gifts are chocolates, cakes, or brandy.
- Gift taboos include: clocks (associated with death), knives (negative connotations), green hats (a Chinese wearing a green hat indicates that his wife or girlfriend has been unfaithful), blankets (suppress prosperity), or handkerchiefs (symbolize grief and parting).
- Never give cash.
- Do not take cameras to give as gifts. Chinese customs officials will make note of any cameras you bring into the country. You will be expected to leave with the same.
- Be conscious of the importance of "numbers" when giving gifts. Do not give gifts that are four in number or that add up to four (such as two pairs of socks).
- Gifts are often given in pairs.
- Gifts in sets of 2, 6, or eight are good. Eight is considered particularly auspicious.

FOR WOMEN

- Less than 10% of the top decision makers in the Chinese government are women.
- Only a small percentage of Chinese women are in managerial positions.
- Foreign businesswomen will have no problem being accepted and will be treated graciously. The "foreign" designation will provide special status.
- Because age and rank are important to the Chinese, if a foreign businesswoman is young, she will need to have strong credentials and connections.

USEFUL ADDRESSES

China World Trade Center Ltd.
Level 7
China World Office
No. 1, Jian Guo Men Wai Avenue
Beijing 100004
People's Republic of China

Fax: (86 10) 65051002
Tel: (86 10) 65052288
Website: http://www.cwtc.com

YOUR CULTURAL IQ

Q **In what country is English the primary language of business, although it is not the mother tongue of any of the residents?**

A English is the primary language used in business, administration, commerce, and tourism in Singapore. It is considered the unifying factor between the three primary ethnic groups: Chinese, Malay, and Indian.

Q **In what cultures would offering another person (even a spouse) food from your plate be considered offensive?**

A The Indian culture believes that once food touches your plate it becomes immediately "polluted" or "tainted".

HONG KONG

THE COUNTRY

Population

- 6.3 million – one of the world's most densely populated areas

Government

- Hong Kong returned to Chinese sovereignty at the stroke of midnight on July 1, 1997. It is now a Special Administrative Region of China (SAR) with a high degree of autonomy, and operates under an arrangement known as "One Country, Two Systems".
- Hong Kong has retained its own legal, social and economic systems.

Climate

- Sub-tropical climate.
- Spring (March-mid May): Temperature and humidity rising. Average temperature 23C (73F).
- Summer (late May-mid September): Hot and humid. Temperatures up to 33C (91F). Humidity near 95%.
- Autumn (late September-early December): Temperature and humidity drop. Average temperature 23C (73F). Humidity near 72%.
- Winter (mid December-February): Cool with low humidity. Temperature can drop to 10C (50F).

Electricity

- 200/220 volts
- Electrical outlets require three-prong round plugs. Most hotels will provide adaptors.

Sports

- Cricket, soccer, ping pong, squash, tennis, swimming and boating.
- Horseracing is a popular spectator sport.

Currency

- *Hong Kong dollar* (HK$)

BUSINESS HOURS

Business & Government Offices

- Most of Hong Kong follows a five or 5 + day workweek.
- Monday through Friday: 9:00 a.m. to 5:00 p.m.
- Saturday: 9:00 a.m. to 1:00 p.m.
- Lunch hour is usually 1:00 p.m. to 2:00 p.m.

Foreign Companies

- Often operate on a five-day workweek.
- Monday to Friday: 9:00 a.m. to 5:00 p.m.

Banks

- Monday to Friday: 9:00 or 9:30 a.m. to 4:00 or 4:30 p.m. (may vary according to branch).
- Saturday: 9:00 a.m. or 9:30 a.m. to 12:00 noon or 12:30 p.m.

Department Stores

- Open daily: 10:00 a.m. to 6:00 p.m. (Central district)
- Open daily: 10:00 a.m. to 9:00 p.m. (Wanchai, Causeway Bay, Tsim Sha Tsui)

HOLIDAYS & FESTIVALS

New Year's Day....................January 1
Chinese Lunar New Year............Late January or early February*
Second day of the Lunar New Year............Late January or early February*
Third day of the Lunar New Year............Late January or early February*
Good Friday....................April*
Day following Good Friday....................April*
Easter Monday....................April*
Ching Ming Festival....................April*
Labour Day....................May 1
Buddha's Birthday....................May*
Tuen Ng Festival....................June*
Hong Kong Special Administrative Region Establishment Day....................July 1
Day following Mid-Autumn Festival....................September/October*
National Day....................October*
Chung Yeung Festival....................October
Christmas Day....................December 25
First weekday after Christmas Day....................December 26

*date varies

THE PEOPLE

Ethnic Groups

- Hong Kong is ethnically homogenous with 95% being Chinese, primarily Cantonese.
- 5% are foreigners.

Language

- Two official languages: Chinese and English
- Cantonese is the most common dialect used, although Mandarin (the official language of Mainland China) is being taught in schools.

Religion

- There is no official religion in Hong Kong.
- Major religions and philosophies are Buddhism, Taoism, and Confucianism.
- Christianity, Hinduism, Sihism, and Judaism are also practiced.
- Ancestor worship, animism, and *feng shui* (the study of wind and water) are often practiced in combination with these religions.

CONDUCTING BUSINESS

Meeting & Greeting

- Businessmen and women greet one another with a handshake that is normally quite light and may last up to 10 seconds.
- Business cards are essential and liberally exchanged. To create a positive impression, have your cards printed in Chinese on the reverse side.
- Cards should be presented and received using both hands. This is often accompanied by a slight nod of the head.
- To show respect, take time to examine the card before storing it away in the appropriate card case/holder.
- It is important to recognize the most senior or elderly person in the group.
- Although Hong Kong professionals are more conscious of time than other Asians and will likely begin business discussions quickly, it is important to begin with polite conversation consisting of inquiries into one's health or activities.
- Meetings generally take place on time as punctuality is important.
- Tea may be served during a meeting. Do not drink until your host takes the first sip.
- Meetings should be scheduled prior to your arrival, and should be made as far ahead as possible.
- Confirm meetings on or near the designated day.
- Relationships and connections, *guanxi*, are an important element of business success.

Forms of Address

- The business culture is formal. Address Chinese using the appropriate courtesy (Mr., Mrs, or Miss) or professional title (President, Doctor) followed by the family name.
- The title "Ms" is used.
- It is appropriate to ask how someone wishes to be addressed.
- Chinese names consist of the family name, which is written first, followed by two (or sometimes one) personal names.
- Many Chinese are adopting Western first names for business. Example: Miss Annie Wu.
- Chinese wives do not take their husband's surname. They should be addressed using their maiden name.

ENTERTAINING

- Business entertaining generally takes place over lunch or dinner. Breakfasts are not common.
- Entertain in high quality restaurants and banquet halls. Facilities are often available at five-star hotels.
- When Hong Kong businesspeople entertain it is normally at a restaurant. You will rarely, if ever, be invited to their homes.
- Spouses are rarely included in business entertaining.
- Chinese banquets are expected to be impressive and are an integral part of doing business in Hong Kong.
- If invited to dinner, it is appropriate to bring a small tasteful gift or alternatively offer to reciprocate with a dinner.
- The tables at traditional restaurants are round with the food normally placed in the center so that guests can serve themselves. At very formal banquets, all courses will be served.
- Seating is important at banquets. The guest of honour will be seated facing the entrance.
- At the end of the dinner, it is customary for the guest of honour to thank the host on behalf of the group being entertained.
- Guests usually leave immediately after a dinner banquet.
- Although it will not be accepted, it is considered polite to offer to pay the bill. Do not offer to split the bill as this would result in loss of face for your host.

DINING ETIQUETTE

- Make an attempt to use your chopsticks. It will enhance your image with your hosts.
- Pace your eating as banquets are long, consisting of eight to twelve courses.
- Do not eat or drink until your host has started.
- Rice is considered a filler. Do not eat large amounts as this will imply that there was an inadequate amount of food served.
- Use the reverse end of your chopsticks for picking up food from serving dishes if a separate spoon is not provided.
- Do not take the last portion from any dish.
- Use your chopstick rests. Do not leave your chopsticks standing straight up in your rice bowl as this reminds the Chinese of a death ritual.
- Tea is the conventional beverage served. Your cup will be constantly replenished. To signal the waiter that a pot refill is required, leave the teapot lid upside down. To indicate you are finished, leave your cup full.
- Toasting is an important part of the dining ritual. Be prepared to reciprocate a toast if the banquet has been held in your honour. Toasts can be made when a new dish is served.
- To signal a waiter for the bill in a restaurant, make a writing motion with your hands.

PUNCTUALITY

- Arrive for meetings on time; it is improper to be late.
- Guests should arrive on time for banquets.

USEFUL PHRASES

Hello (telephone)
Wai
(Why)

Good morning
Jou sahn
(Jo sun)

Good afternoon
Ngh on
(Ng awn)

Good bye
Joigin
(Joy-geen)

Thank you
Dojeh
(Dor-ts-yeh)

Yes
Haih
(High)

No
Mh-haih
(Mm-high)

How are you?
Nieh hou ma?
(Nee how ma?)

VALUES AND SOCIAL CONVENTIONS

- Family is an integral part of life in Hong Kong. Family honour is important.
- Education is highly valued.
- Hong Kong Chinese are very conscious of social position and status.
- The pace of life is very fast and hectic. Hong Kong Chinese are entrepreneurial and hard-working.
- Monetary gain is the primary motivator.
- Do not directly criticize anyone. Causing an individual to "lose face" impacts the entire family causing shame or dishonour.
- A loud tone of voice should be avoided.
- It is common to be asked personal questions. It is acceptable to refrain from responding if you are uncomfortable.
- Laughing or smiling may conceal feelings of embarrassment.
- Rather than say "no", the Chinese are more comfortable indicating something is difficult, under consideration or untimely.
- "Yes" may indicate "I hear you" rather than "I agree".
- Eating while walking on the street is frowned upon.
- It is important to be colour conscious. Some colours indicate good fortune, while others signify bad luck.
- Examples: black is associated with death (should not be used as the border of a card or page). Do not use a red ink pen for signatures, as red ink is associated with the severance of relationships.
- Be conscious of the colours used in marketing and presentation materials, gift wrapping and clothing.
- The Chinese are superstitious regarding numbers. When planning events, it is recommended that you discuss dates, numbers of guests, etc. with your Hong Kong partners to ensure that the numbers are favourable.
- The number four is considered unlucky as the word for "four" sounds like the word for "death".

BODY LANGUAGE

- To beckon an individual, extend your hand, palm down, and make a scratching motion towards the body.
- The Chinese do not normally display affection in public, including holding hands with the opposite sex.
- Pointing should be done with an open hand. Do not point with your index finger.
- When sitting, place your hands in your lap. Women may cross their legs, but it is considered inappropriate for men to do so.
- The Chinese are uncomfortable with body contact. Do not hug, kiss or pat people on the back.
- Avoid winking as it is considered a rude gesture.

CONVERSATION

- Avoid discussions about poverty, failure or death.
- Acceptable topics includes general inquiries about one's health, business conditions, the excellent cuisine, and shopping.

TIPPING

- Tipping is common and expected.
- Restaurants: 5 to 10% in addition to the standard service charge.
- Taxi drivers: 10% of the fare
- Doormen and porters: minimum HK $5 per item.
- Concierges: minimum HK $10

DRESS & APPEARANCE

- Business suits in dark colours for men. Hong Kong men are normally very well groomed: brand name shoes, shirts, and ties.
- Fashion in Hong Kong is especially prized and respected. Designer labels are popular.
- Women would therefore be wise to invest in high quality and classic styling clothing. It is important to be well-dressed and well-groomed. Skirt suits are preferred. Carrying a briefcase is considered stylish and prestigious.
- Avoid wearing blue or white to social events as these colours are associated with death and mourning.

GIFTS

- Gifts are not normally exchanged during initial encounters, although small items such as gourmet chocolates or handicrafts are appreciated.
- Once a relationship has been established, however, gifts are customary and it important to follow the appropriate etiquette.
- Gifts should be presented and received with both hands.
- Giving a pair (two) of any item is considered auspicious.
- Gifts should be elegantly wrapped in red, green or gold paper.
- Do not wrap gifts in the colours of white, black or blue.
- The recipient of a gift never opens it in the presence of the person who gave it, but politely puts it aside to be opened later.
- The Chinese will normally refuse a gift three times before accepting. Persist in offering the gift until they accept.
- Avoid giving clocks (associated with death) , knives (suggest the severing of relationships), handkerchiefs (symbolize grief), green hats (indicates the recipient's wife or girlfriend has been unfaithful), blankets (suppress prosperity) and white flowers (associated with mourning).

FOR WOMEN

- Gender is not an obstacle to doing business in Hong Kong.
- Hong Kong women have attained a high level of prominence in the business world.

USEFUL ADDRESSES

World Trade Center Hong Kong
8/F Asia Pacific Center
8 Wyndham Street
Central, Hong Kong
Fax: (852) 2577 9708
Tel: (852) 2894 8083

YOUR CULTURAL IQ

Q

In which countries is punctuality for business meetings important?

A

Although some countries have a relaxed attitude towards time, foreign business people should to be punctual for meetings in all countries.

Q

Why would patting a child on the head cause a mother to become upset?

A

In many Asian countries, there is a belief that the spirit or soul resides in a person's head.

INDIA

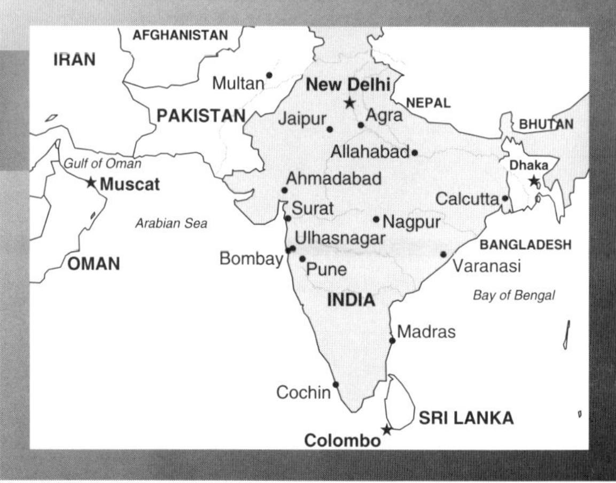

THE COUNTRY

Population

- 936 million
- India is the second most populous country in the world.
- 1/6th of the world's people lives in India.

Capital

- New Delhi (7.1 million)

Major Cities

- Bombay (9.9 million)
- Calcutta (4.4 million)

Government

- Multiparty Federal Republic

Climate

- Generally, there are three main seasons: cool winter from October to February; hot summer from March to June; and the rainy monsoon season from July to September.
- Temperatures normally do not go below 4C (40F) in January and will reach uncomfortable temperatures as high as 45C (113F) during the summer (even in the northern areas).
- The southern region is generally the warmest in any season.

Electricity

- 220 volts
- Electrical outlets require two-pin, round-headed plugs.

Sports

- Soccer, cricket, tennis and field hockey.

Currency

- Indian *rupee* (Rs.)

BUSINESS HOURS

Business Offices and Banks

- Monday to Friday: 9:30 a.m. to 1:00 p.m. and 2:00 p.m. to 5:00 p.m.
- Some businesses may be open for a half or full day on Saturdays.
- Hours for rural areas may differ.

Government Offices

- Monday to Saturday: 10:00 a.m. to 5:00 p.m.
- Closed for lunch from 1:00 p.m. to 2:00 p.m.
- Closed every second Saturday of each month.

HOLIDAYS & FESTIVALS

- Each state or region has local holidays. Business is not conducted during religious holidays.
- Check with the Indian Tourist Office, Consulate, or Embassy before travelling.

International New Year's Day........... January 1
Republic Day..January 26
Ramadan...*
Eid-ul-Fitr (Ramazan Eid)..................................*
Holi..March*
Annual closing of bank accounts...........April 1
Easter and Good Friday.................March/April*
Eid-ul-Zuha (Feast of sacrifice).....May/June*
Muharram......................................July/August*
Independence Day..............................August 15
Half year closing of
bank accounts...........................September 30
Durga Puja Dussera.........September/October*
Mahatma Gandhi's Birthday
(Gandi Jayanti)................................October 2
Diwali
(Festival of Lights)........October/November*
Guru Nanak's
Birthday.......................November/December*
Christmas Day...............................December 25

*date varies

THE PEOPLE

Ethnic Groups

- 72% are Indo-Aryans
- 25% Dravidians
- 3% Mongoloid and Australoid
- One of the most culturally diverse countries in the world.
- Primarily rural with 70% subsistence farmers.

Language

- More than three hundred languages are spoken; 24 of these have one million or more speakers.
- There are 14 official languages including: Hindi, English, Bengali, Urdu, Punjabi, and Sanskrit.
- 30% of the population speak Hindi.
- English is the language of commerce and administration.

Religion

- More than 82% of the population are Hindu; 11% are Muslims. Other major religions include: Christianity, Sikhism, Buddhism, Zoroastrianism, and Jainism.
- India has the third largest Muslim population in the world.
- There is no official religion.

CONDUCTING BUSINESS

Meeting & Greeting

- Try to schedule all appointments at least two months in advance keeping in mind that the Indian mail to rural areas is slow and unreliable. This however does not apply in the major cities. The telephone system often makes faxing difficult. Courier service may be required, or send communications via e-mail.
- Avoid scheduling appointments before 10:00 a.m. or over the lunch period between 1:00 p.m. and 2:00 p.m. Late mornings or early afternoons are the preferred meeting times for Indian executives.
- Contact should be made with the most senior executive as decisions are made at the top level.
- Most Indians will greet one another with a handshake or *namaste* (na-mas-tay) which is done by holding the palms of your hands together (as in a prayer) below the chin, accompanied by a slight nod.
- Do not use the left hand for greeting or saying goodbye to Muslims.
- Many Indians will not shake a woman's hand. This is a sign of respect for a woman's privacy. It is important that a woman waits for a man to initiate a handshake.
- Business cards are exchanged at the first meeting.
- English is acceptable for business cards. Academic credentials and professional affiliations may be added to your business card. Indians are impressed by status.
- Use Hindi for promotional literature to increase your market.
- Tea, coffee, or soft drinks are often served prior to the start of the meeting. It is customary to refuse the first offer and accept on the second or third. To completely refuse is considered insulting.
- Do not begin talking business immediately. Small talk on topics such as your impressions of India is important for building relationships.
- Business generally proceeds rather slowly. Be patient.

Forms of Address

- Use professional titles (Doctor, professor) or the English courtesy titles (Mr., Mrs. or Miss) plus the family name unless familiar with the Hindu, Muslim or Sikh greeting customs. Wait until invited to use first names.

Hindu:

- Given names come first, followed by family names.
- It is polite to use professional titles or *Shri* (Mr.); *Shrimati* (Mrs.) or *Kumari* (Miss) or the suffix – *ji* with a last name to show respect.

Muslim:

- Muslims have no surname. A Muslim is generally known by a given name followed by *bin* (son of) or *binti* (daughter of) plus the father's given name.
- Married Muslim women do not always take the husband's name.

Sikhs:

- The given name is always followed by either *Singh* (for males) or *Kaur* (for females).
- All Sikhs use the name *Singh,* but not all Singhs are Sikhs.
- Address Sikhs by their professional title or Mr., Mrs., or Miss, and by their first name.
- To address a Sikh male as Mr. Singh is the equivalent of saying "Mr. Man" in English.

ENTERTAINING

- Indians are generally very gracious and hospitable hosts.
- Business socializing normally occurs over dinner. India's heat, humidity and traffic limit lunches. Breakfasts are uncommon.
- Entertaining is generally done in prestigious hotels, restaurants or private clubs.
- Business is often discussed over meals. Wait for your host to initiate the discussion.
- The guest of honour should be seated to the right of the host. There are no other seating formalities.
- In some traditional homes, seating may consist of floor mats at low tables.
- In rural homes, the women may be seated separately.
- Many Indians do not wear shoes in the home. Ask if you should remove your shoes.
- The Continental style of eating (fork in left hand, knife in right) is used in most Westernized restaurants.
- Never refuse an invitation. It is best to respond with "I will try".

DINING ETIQUETTE

- Hindus and Sikhs do not eat beef. Many are vegetarians.
- Muslims eat beef, but do not eat pork or shellfish.
- All Orthodox Muslims and most Hindus do not consume alcohol.
- When offered food or a beverage, it is considered polite to initially refuse and then accept.
- In hotels, restaurants and many homes, utensils will be provided. However, if your hosts eat with their hands, you should do the same. Use the tips of your first three fingers and the thumb of your right hand only. Wrap pieces of bread around meat, vegetables and sauces.
- Do not serve yourself. Wait for the host to serve you.
- Always use a serving spoon, rather than your fingers, to take food from a communal dish.
- It is offensive to offer food (even to a family member) from your plate to others. It is considered polluted as soon as it touches your plate.
- Orthodox Hindus will not allow people outside their caste or religion touch their food.
- Always wash your hands before a meal. In Hindu homes, you will be expected to also wash out your mouth.
- After eating to aid digestion, it is customary to be served *pan,* a mixture of spices rolled in a betel leaf.
- The party that extends the invitation always pays for the meal.

PUNCTUALITY

- Although Indians appreciate punctuality, many are not on time for appointments and do not mind if foreign visitors are up to fifteen minutes late. Try to maintain a flexible schedule.
- If invited to a home for dinner, it is appropriate to arrive fifteen to thirty minutes late.
- For dinners outside the home, arrive a few minutes late unless it is an official government function.

USEFUL PHRASES

- If you know or are able to determine the person's religion, the appropriate greetings should be used:
- **Hindu greeting and response:** Namaste *(nah-mahss-tay)* or Namaskar *(nah-mahss-car)* (I pay my respects to you)
- **Muslim greeting:** Salam Alaikum *(sah-laam a-lie-come)* (Peace be upon you)
- **Response:** Vaalaikum Salaam *(vah-lie-come- sah-laam)* (And peace be upon you also)
- **Sikh greeting and response:** Sat Sri Akal *(sut-sree-ah-kaal)* (Truth is eternal)

Note: When in doubt, use English words such as "Pleased to meet you".

VALUES AND SOCIAL CONVENTIONS

- Values, language, food, dress, and other cultural elements of Indians will vary according to religion and geographical location.
- Religion is central to daily life.
- The ideals of humility and self-denial are highly respected.
- The family takes precedence over the individual.
- The elderly are respected and cared for by their families.
- Traditional marriages are still arranged by parents.
- Although the complex and diverse Hindu caste system has been constitutionally abolished, it continues to play an important role in politics and business. There are four major castes and many subcastes. Below the fourth caste are the "untouchables" or "Dalits" (meaning oppressed people). The most affluent and influential Indians are from one of the higher castes.
- Because of the Hindu influence, there is a strong belief in fate or *karma.* There is therefore an acceptance that one's destiny has been predetermined and there are limits to what can be changed.
- Indians do not use the usual courtesy words such as "Please" and "thank you". They do not intend to be rude. Most Indian languages do not have translations for these words. In addition, there is the belief that routine courtesies do not require gratitude. Indians will perform functions out of a sense of duty.
- Excessive use of the word "thank you" may be perceived as insincere.
- Indians will not say "no" directly as it has harsh implications. "I will try" is considered the more polite answer.
- Because of a strong belief in the "evil eye" (anything beautiful and attractive will catch the attention of the evil eye) it is important not to compliment children.
- Tipping or *"baksheesh"* (grease money) in India may not always be a reward for good service, but a way of getting things done i.e. to ensure a train seat.

BODY LANGUAGE

- Public displays of affection are strictly frowned upon. Do not hug, touch, or kiss in greeting.
- Never touch a woman except to shake hands.
- Some Muslims believe that if a man is touched by a woman, he must ritually cleanse before he can pray again.
- In initial encounters, men should avoid physical contact with their Indian host.
- Indian men hold hands or link arms as a sign of friendship.
- As feet are thought of as unclean, it is considered an insult to touch a person with your feet or shoes. To remove an offense, immediately apologize. Feet should be kept flat on the floor.
- Do not point using a single finger. Use the palm of your hand, chin, or thumb.
- To beckon someone, put your hand out, palm side down, and make a scratching motion towards you.
- Whistling is considered impolite.
- Do not sniff or handle flowers at a market. It is considered impolite.
- For many Indians, the head is the most sacred part of the body since it houses the soul. Do not touch anyone's head, even to pat the head of a child.
- Indians will indicate *yes* by moving their heads in a figure eight or by smiling and jerking their head back.
- Do not wink at women. It is considered demeaning.
- Since the left hand is considered unclean, do not use it for eating, touching anyone, receiving gifts, or picking up merchandise.
- Ears are considered sacred. Grasping an earlobe indicates sincerity or repentance.
- An Indian may indicate acceptance or understanding by tossing his head from side to side.
- Maintain an arm's length distance from someone of the opposite sex. Indians value personal space.

CONVERSATION

- Indians enjoy discussing their flourishing motion picture industry (one of the world's largest), travel, sports, and their rich artistic and architectural heritage.
- Avoid personal questions or discussing India's poverty, politics or religion.

TIPPING

- Restaurants: 10% of the bill in major hotels and restaurants; 5% in moderately priced establishments.
- Taxi drivers: Pay by Meter Card.
- Private car drivers: Rs. 25 for a half day to Rs. 50 for a full day.
- Porters: Rs. 5 per bag
- Tour guides: Rs. 5 to Rs. 10
- Shoe guardian at temples: couple of Rupees.

DRESS & APPEARANCE

- For business, men should wear a suit and tie. The jacket may be omitted in hot summer weather. Women should wear conservative pant suits or dresses.
- For casual occasions, men should wear cotton shirts and pants. Women should wear modest clothing, covering up as much of the body as comfort permits, particularly in Muslim areas.
- Indians are flattered when a foreign woman wants to wear a *sari*. Be sure to receive instructions on how to wear it correctly.
- Shorts should be avoided except at beaches and for athletic activities. Women should wear long pants jogging.
- Wearing leather (belts and handbags) may be offensive to some religious Indians, especially in temples.

GIFTS

- In business, gifts are not usually exchanged at initial meetings. Upon the completion of a deal, however, it is considered acceptable to give something of quality from your home country.
- Do not give gifts made of cowhide (i.e. leather picture frames). Cows are looked upon as sacred and the killing of them is equivalent to murdering a human being.
- Gifts are not opened in the presence of the giver.
- Wrapping should be done in the lucky colours of green, red, or yellow. Avoid wrapping in the unlucky colours of black or white.
- If invited to an Indian's home for dinner it is polite to bring a small gift such as chocolates, fruit, flowers (except frangipani blossoms as they are associated with mourning) or candy.

FOR WOMEN

- Although there are successful Indian women in business and government, women are still considered inferior to men.
- India is a difficult and challenging country for a foreign woman to do business.
- Employing an agent is helpful.
- It is important that a woman establish her credentials. Sending a biography ahead of time, as well as including her position, academic credentials, and professional affiliations on a business card, may assist.
- A foreign woman may entertain an Indian man at a business meal. Most men will offer to pay the bill, but the she should insist upon paying.
- Women should never wink or whistle.

USEFUL ADDRESSES

World Trade Centre Mumbai
Centre 1, 31st Floor
Cuffe Parade
Mumbai 400 005
India
Telephone: (91 22) 218 4434
Fax: (91 22) 218 8385/218 8175
Email: wtcbom@giasbm01.vsnl.net.in

YOUR CULTURAL IQ

Q **In what culture would using your left hand for eating be considered disgusting?**

A In the Muslim culture, the left hand is considered "unclean".

Q **In what country would the North American gesture for "victory", a "V" formed with the index and middle finger, be misinterpreted?**

A This gesture, if the palm is facing towards you, is considered vulgar in Australia.

INDONESIA

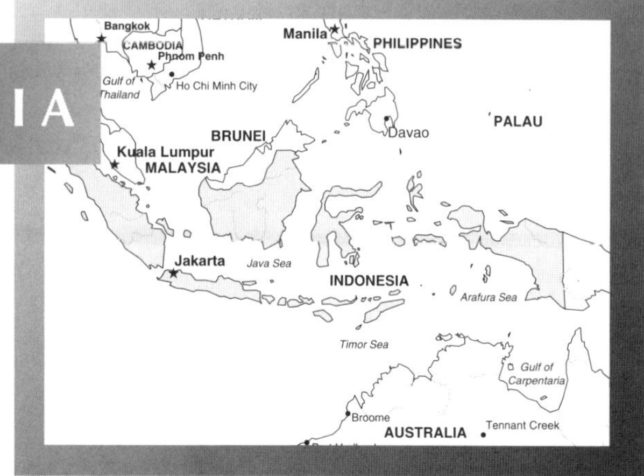

THE COUNTRY

Population
- 212 million
- It is the fourth most populous country in the world.
- Approximately 70% of its people live in rural areas.

Capital
- Jakarta (8.6 million)

Major Cities
- Surabaya (2.5 million)
- Medan (1.8 million)
- Bandung (2.9 million)

Government
- Unitary multiparty republic.
- President is both head of state and head of the government.

Climate
- Indonesia has a hot and humid equatorial climate. The rainy season is from November to March. Heaviest rains are received in December and January. Temperatures average between 23C (74F) and 30C (85F).
- April to October is the dry season, with temperatures averaging between 23C (74F) and 31C (88F).

Electricity
- Both 220 volts and 110 volts are used.
- Electrical outlets require plugs with two thin round pins.

Sports
- Soccer, volleyball, tennis and bicycling. Indonesians are among the best in the world in badminton.

Currency
- The *rupiah* (pronounced rupee) Rp

BUSINESS HOURS

Business Offices
- Monday to Friday: 8:00 a.m. or 9:00 a.m. to 4:00 or 5:00 p.m.
- Saturday: 8:00 a.m. or 9:00 a.m. to 12:00 noon or 1:00 p.m
- Some offices close at midday on Friday for Muslim worship.
- Most close for an hour or two in the afternoon.

Government Offices
- Monday to Thursday: 8:00 a.m. to 3:00 p.m.
- Friday: 8:00 a.m. to 11:30 a.m.
- Saturday: 8:00 a.m. to 2:00 p.m.

Banks
- Monday to Friday: 8:00 a.m. to 12:00 noon or 2:00 p.m.
- Some are open on Saturdays.
- Hotel bank branches may stay open later each day.

Stores
- Monday to Saturday: 8:00 a.m. to 9:00 p.m.
- Some are open for part of the day on Sunday.

HOLIDAYS & FESTIVALS

New Year's Day....................January 1
Mi'raj Nabi Muhammad....................*
Ramadan....................*
Nyepi....................March*
Good Friday....................March/April*
Eid-el-Fitr....................*
Eid al-Adha....................*
Waisak....................May*
Isa Amasih....................May*
National Independence Day....................August 17
Maulid Nabi Muhammad....................July*
Christmas Day....................December 25

*date varies

THE PEOPLE

Ethnic Groups

- Indonesia has a very diverse cultural mix, with more than 350 tribal and ethnic groups.

The largest groups are:

- 45% Javanese
- 14% Sudanese
- 7.5% Madurese
- 7.5% Coastal Malays
- 26% various smaller groups

Language

- The official language is Bahasa Indonesian (a form of Malay).
- Javanese is the second most common language.
- More than 300 other languages are spoken.
- English is the leading international language.

Religion

- 87% of Indonesians are Muslim.
- Indonesia has the largest Muslim population in the world.

CONDUCTING BUSINESS

Meeting & Greeting

- Greetings in Indonesia are very formal and should not be rushed.
- When first meeting an Indonesian man or woman, the appropriate greeting is to shake hands accompanied by a slight nod and a smile.
- The Indonesian handshake is relatively soft and lingering.
- Unless there has been a long separation, for subsequent meetings handshakes are not common. A slight bow or nod of the head is more appropriate.
- Because of the Muslim influence, after shaking hands, many Indonesians will bring their hands back to the chest to indicate that the greeting is from the heart.
- As most Indonesians are either Muslim or Hindu, there is minimal physical contact between sexes. You may see members of the opposite sex walk hand-in-hand in only the major cities.
- Women should not offer to shake the hands of an Indonesian man. The Islamic faith dictates that if a man is touched by a woman he must ritually cleanse before praying again.
- Foreign women should wait for an Indonesian man to offer his hand before shaking it. Foreign men should also wait for an Indonesian woman to offer her hand.
- A Westernized Indonesian man will offer to shake the hands of a foreign woman.
- Women may use the *namaste* greeting as an alternative when greeting Hindu men. This involves putting the hands together at chest level, as in a prayer, and bowing slightly.
- Chinese men will shake hands with both men and women. A bow may accompany the handshake.
- The traditional Indonesian greeting is *"Selamat"* (pronounced S'lah-maht) which means peace.
- Indonesians are impressed by credentials and position, so be sure to include academic degrees or professional certifications on your business card.
- Business cards should be printed in English. You may wish to have Chinese printed on the reverse on some of your cards.
- Use your right hand (lightly supported by your left hand) or both hands for giving and receiving business cards.
- Be sure to have the print on the card facing the direction of the recipient.
- Treat all cards with respect. After receiving a card, examine it closely before storing it away in the appropriate business card holder or inside jacket pocket. Do not store cards in a back pocket.
- Never write on a person's business card while in their presence.
- Meetings should begin with casual conversation on topics such as the weather, your travels, sports, or Indonesian culture.
- It is appropriate to say *Terima kasih* "thank you" at the end of every meeting.
- The Indonesian rhetorical greeting, *"Have you eaten yet"* and *"Have you taken food"* should be answered with an affirmative, whether or not you have had food recently.
- Another popular greeting is *"Where are you going?"* You are not expected to provide information regarding your itinerary. One possible response is *"Nowhere of importance"*.
- Business generally proceeds rather slowly. Be patient.

Forms of Address

- Common people will usually have only one name; members of the middle class will often have two; members of the upper class will have long names.
- Indonesians should be addressed by either their professional title, or the English courtesy titles (Mr., Mrs., Miss) followed by their name.
- It is considered courteous to use the Indonesian traditional titles of *Bapak* (bah-pak) for men which literally means father, or *Ibu* (ee-boo) for females which means "mother". The titles are equivalent to using Mr., Mrs., or Miss. These titles are used in front of an individual's name.
- *Bapak* is sometimes shortened to *pak.*
- The formula for the most formal introduction is as follows:
  - *Bapak/Ibu* +
  - academic title if applicable +
  - noble title if the person normally use it +
  - person's given and family names +
  - business and social position+
  - academic title if you did not use it at the beginning
- This formal method of introduction will be used by very traditional Indonesians that are concerned with the possibility of causing embarrassment should an important title or designation be omitted.
- If a man has completed his pilgrimage to Mecca, he will be addressed as *Haji.*
- If a women has completed her pilgrimage to Mecca, she will be addressed as *Hajah.*
- These honorific titles must be individually earned and usually supersede others.

Chinese:

- In Chinese names, the family name is traditionally placed first, followed by the given name. Individuals should be addressed by Mr., Mrs., or Miss followed by their family name or surname.
- It is common to address the Chinese using their professional or government title followed by their surname.
- Chinese women normally keep their maiden names upon marriage. A married woman should be addressed as Madame (or Mrs.) plus her maiden family name.
- Many Chinese have taken an English first name or use their initials to ease communications with English speakers.

ENTERTAINING

- Business is often conducted over early breakfast meetings. Lunches are not as common. Dinners are primarily for socializing and cementing relationships.
- Spouses may be invited to dinners, but not lunches. Business will not be discussed in their presence.
- If both men and women are present, the male guest of honour will be seated next to the host. The female guest of honour will be seated next to the hostess.
- Due to the Islamic influence, alcohol is rarely consumed in restaurants.
- The meal is always paid for by the inviter. Restaurant bills are not shared.

DINING ETIQUETTE

- Indonesians use a fork and spoon for dining. The spoon is held in the right hand, the fork in the left. The fork is used to push food onto the spoon.
- Fingers may be used instead of cutlery. Eat using the right hand only, making sure to keep your hands on the table at all times.
- Never refuse an offer of food or drink.
- Do not begin drinking until your host has invited you to begin.
- An empty glass indicates a refill is necessary.
- It is best to avoid drinking hard liquor or wine. Beer is acceptable.
- It is considered impolite to completely finish the food on your plate. Always leave a small amount.
- Pass and accept food using your right hand only.
- At the completion of a meal, your fork should be placed, tines down, on the plate. The spoon, face down, should be placed across the fork.
- If entertained in a private home, it is polite to rise when the host or hostess enters the room.
- Follow the lead of the host/hostess with respect to wearing shoes in the home.

PUNCTUALITY

- Indonesians appreciate punctuality, although they may not always be on time.
- The Indonesians often use the phrase *jam karet*, or "rubber time", which reflects their relaxed attitude towards time.
- The general rule is the higher the status of the Indonesian, the more they will appreciate punctuality.
- For social events, most Indonesians will arrive approximately one-half hour late.

USEFUL PHRASES

Yes
Ya
(yah)

No
Tidak
(Teedah)

Please
Silahkan
(Seelakahn)

Thank you
Terima kasih (man)
(T'rrreema kasseehh)

Thank you
Terima kembali (woman)
(T'rreema kembahlee)

You're welcome
Kembali or Sama
(Kembahlee or Sahmah)

Good morning
Selamat pagi
(S'lahmaht pahghee)

Good afternoon
Selamat sore
(S'lahmaht sawrreh)

Good evening
Selamat malam
(S'lahmaht mahlahm)

Goodbye
Selamat tinggal
(s'lahmaht teenggal)

VALUES AND SOCIAL CONVENTIONS

- Status, age, and position are highly respected by Indonesians.
- Elders are revered.
- Relationships are critical to doing business in Indonesia. Spend time establishing your social ties.
- Indonesians smile a lot. They are friendly and eager to please.
- If complimented by an Indonesian, do not simply reply with "thank you". A more humble response such as "thank you, but it was nothing" or something similar is more appropriate.
- It is important to always remain polite and courteous. Considerable value is placed on these attributes.
- Criticism should be avoided. It if must be given, it should be well disguised.
- Indonesians do not consider it polite to say "no" or disagree with someone. Possible alternatives include "yes, but..." or "It might be difficult" or a complete evasion of the question. They will often use the phrase *"Belum"* which means "not yet".
- Do not always assume "yes" indicates an affirmative.
- Do not express anger in public. To do so will lose the respect of Indonesians. You will also be judged as someone who cannot be trusted.
- Indonesians have a preference for refined, subdued, and polite behaviour.
- Indonesians may ask you personal questions. Do not take offense.
- Avoid discussing personal achievements. It is considered impolite and boastful.
- Show considerable respect to elders, civil servants, and superiors.
- Indonesians are comfortable about openly discussing birth control.

BODY LANGUAGE

- Indonesians will often smile or laugh to hide sadness, disappointment or embarrassment. Do not automatically assume that the smile has a positive meaning.
- Avoid touching someone's head (even to pat a child's head) as Indonesians believe it is where the spirit or soul resides.
- Also avoid touching an Indonesian on the back as it is considered a private part of the person.
- Kissing, even a slight peck on the cheek, is not done in public.
- It is common to see people of the same sex holding hands or with arms around each other while walking in public. This is regarded as a sign of friendship.
- For both Muslims and Hindus, the left hand is reserved for personal hygiene and therefore considered unclean. Do not eat, accept gifts, pass objects, or hold cash with your

left hand. When both hands are needed, it is acceptable to use both.

- The foot is also considered unclean. Avoid showing the soles of your feet (or shoes), touching anyone or moving objects with your feet.
- When crossing your legs, do not place one ankle on the other knee.
- Do not chew gum or yawn in public. If you cannot avoid yawning, at least cover your mouth.
- To beckon someone, extend the arm out, hand down, and make a downward scratching motion with your fingers towards your body. Avoid beckoning anyone except for a taxi or a child.
- Standing with your hands on your hips or in your pockets will be perceived by an Indonesian as defiance or arrogance.

CONVERSATION

- Indonesians enjoy discussions about sports, aspects of their culture, travel, their families, and Indonesian cuisine.
- Avoid discussing religion, politics, bureaucracy or human rights records.

TIPPING

- Hotels and restaurants: a 10% service charge is normally included.
- Porters: Rp 500 per item.
- Bellboys and doormen: Rp 2000
- Taxi drivers: A tip of Rp 500 is optional, but common. Or it is acceptable to leave the small change from a bill.
- Washroom attendants: Rp100 to 500.

DRESS & APPEARANCE

- Because Indonesia is hot and humid year round, the business dress of Indonesians is quite casual. Suits are generally not worn by Indonesians except for formal occasions or important meetings.
- As a foreigner, you should dress formally until aware of the degree of informality that is accepted by the people you are visiting.
- For business, men should wear jackets, ties, and dress trousers. For women, skirts, blouses (always with sleeves) or dresses are acceptable. Avoid bright colours and flamboyant fashions. Dark and muted colours are more appropriate.
- Women should adhere to the Muslim deference to modesty.
- An invitation stating "Lounge suits" for men implies a standard Western style suit.

GIFTS

- Gift giving is an important aspect of doing business in Indonesia.
- Gifts are presented upon the conclusion of a business transaction, when invited to an Indonesian home, to celebrate an occasion or to reward services rendered.
- The recipient of a gift never opens it in the presence of the person who gave it, but politely puts it aside to be opened later.
- Suitable gifts can range from ties, household appliances, silk scarves, leather bags (as long as they are not pigskin) to food.
- Do not give alcohol or food items containing pork.
- Pictures of dogs, or toy dogs, should not be given. Muslim Indonesians consider dogs unclean.
- Personal gifts should not be given by a man to a woman, or the reverse. A romantic misinterpretation may result.

Hindu:

- Do not give any leather products, as cows are considered sacred.

Chinese:

- The Chinese will normally refuse a gift three times before accepting. Persist in offering the gift until they accept.
- Avoid giving clocks (associated with death) , knives (suggest the severing of relationships), handkerchiefs (symbolize grief), green hats (indicates the recipient's wife or girlfriend has been unfaithful), blankets (suppress prosperity) and white flowers (associated with mourning).
- Giving a pair (two) of any item is considered auspicious.
- Do not wrap gifts in the colours of white, black or blue.

FOR WOMEN

- Foreign women will have little trouble conducting business in Indonesia.
- Indonesian women have been active in business and government for many years.
- A foreign businesswomen may invite a male Indonesian to dinner. She should indicate that the invitation is on behalf of her company. To avoid embarrassing her guest, she should make arrangements for payment in advance.

USEFUL ADDRESSES

World Trade Centre Jakarta
World Trade Center Bldg., 2nd floor
Jl. Jend. Sudirman Kav. 29-31
Jakarta, 12920, Indonesia

Fax: (62 21) 252 2135/571 1673
Tel: (62 21) 521 1125/252 1126

World Trade Centre Medan
BMW House, L. 3, Jalan H. Adam
Malik 161
Medan, North Sumatra
Indonesia 20114

Fax: (62 61) 618 4092
Tel: (62 61) 618 401/618 403
Email: mardian@idola.net.id

World Trade Centre Surabaya
Jalan Pemuda 27-31
Surabaya 60271
Indonesia

Fax: (62 31) 519 287
Telephone: (62 31) 519 310/311/312
Website:
http://www.rad.net.id/wtc-su/

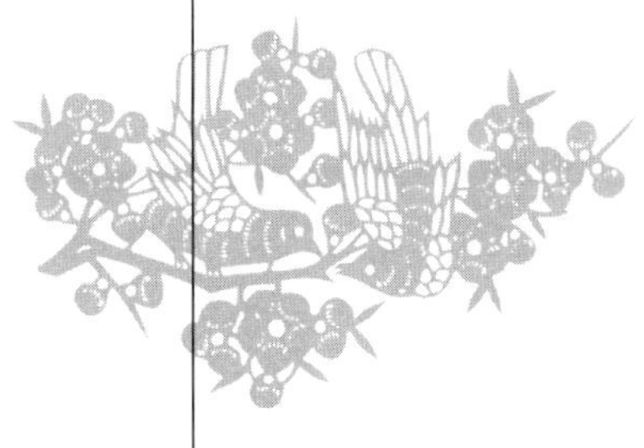

JAPAN

THE COUNTRY

Population
- 126 million
- One of the most densely populated countries in the world.

Capital
- Tokyo (11.6 million)
- One of the most populous cities in the world.

Major Cities
- Osaka (2.6 million)
- Nagoya (2.2 million)
- Sapporo (1.8 million)
- Kyoto (1.5 million)

Government
- Parliamentary democracy under a constitutional monarch.
- The emperor is the symbol of state.

Climate
- Japan has four distinct seasons.
- Weather patterns vary across the country.
- The climate conditions for Tokyo are as follows:
- Summers are hot and humid, with temperatures ranging between 26C (80F) and 35C (95F).
- Winters are cold and dry. Temperatures range between –1C (30F) and 10C (50F).
- The rainy season occurs from mid-June to mid-July.

Electricity
- Both 100 and 200 volts used.
- Outlets require plugs with two flat prongs.

Sports
- Golf is an extremely popular recreation among businessmen and women.
- Other prevalent sports include baseball, tennis, football, soccer, and skiing.
- Sumo wrestling is a popular spectator sport.

Currency
- The *Yen* (Y)

BUSINESS HOURS

Business & Government Offices
- Monday to Friday: 9:00 a.m. to 5:00 p.m or 6:00 p.m.
- Some companies operate a half-day on Saturdays.
- Many white-collar professionals (salarymen) work late into the evening (as late as 12:00 midnight)

Banks
- Monday to Friday: 9:00 a.m. to 3:00 p.m.

Stores
- Department stores, open daily: 10:00 a.m. to 7:00 p.m. or 7:30 p.m.
- Supermarkets, open daily: 10:00 a.m. to 11:00 p.m. or 12:30 p.m.

HOLIDAYS & FESTIVALS

Come of Age Day	January 15
Adults' Day	January 15
National Foundation Day	February 11
Spring Equinox	Around March 21*
Greenery Day	April 29
Constitution Day	May 3
National Holiday	May 4
Children's Day	May 5
Marine Day	July 20
Obon Festival	August*
Respect for the Aged Day	September 15
Autumnal Equinox	Around September 23*
Physical Fitness Day	October 10
Sports Day	October 15
Cultural Day	November 3
Labour Thanksgiving Day	November 23
Emperor's Birthday	December 23
New Year's Holidays	Around December 29 to January 3

*date varies

- Holidays that fall upon a Sunday are observed the following day.
- Businesses are usually closed during the period from December 29 to January 4.
- Many Japanese take holidays during the month of August.
- Many Japanese will visit the graves of their ancestors during the Obon which is held in mid-August.
- Avoid scheduling meetings during the Obon, New Year's holidays, December 28 to January 4, and Golden Week, April 29 to May 5.
- Although banks and offices close during holidays, some stores stay open for business.

THE PEOPLE

Ethnic Groups

- More than 99% of the population are Japanese.
- It is one of the most homogenous populations in the world.
- Remaining 1% consist of three minority ethnic groups: people of Korean descent (mostly descendants of labourers imported during World War II); Ainu, the aboriginal people of the Hokkaido; and Okinawans.
- 70% of the population live along the coastal plain between Tokyo and the northern part of Kyushu (includes the major cities of Yokohama, Osaka, Nagoya and Kobe).

Language

- The official language is Japanese.

Religion

- Japan has no official religion. Although Shintoism, Buddhism, Christianity, and Confucian philosophy are practiced.
- Approximately 87% are adherents of Shintoism, a religion unique to Japan.
- Shintoism as well as Confucian thought have been important in forming Japanese social values.

CONDUCTING BUSINESS

Meeting & Greeting

- The traditional form of greeting is the bow. Bowing may also be used to convey gratitude.
- The bow is used to show respect towards others as well as indicate personal humility.
- The depth of the bow and placement of the hands (either on the sides of the body or with palms flat on the thighs) indicates the formality of the occasion and the degree of respect.
- The points below are a simplification of the complicated art of bowing, but will provide some initial guidance.
- The informal bow is used for casual occasions between individuals of all ranks. The depth of the bow is about 15 degrees, with hands on either side of the body, and eyes always facing the floor.
- It is preferred that more junior person always bows first and lower.
- The formal bow is always used at initial meetings.
- The most formal bow is used towards individuals of greater rank or age. The palms of the hands are flat on the thighs, eyes are facing the floor, and the depth of the bow is about 45 degrees.
- A respectful nod of the head and shoulders is acceptable if a foreign visitor has not mastered the art of bowing.
- Many Japanese have started to greet foreign visitors with a handshake and a bow.
- Keep your handshake light as the Japanese grip will be quite soft and limp.
- There is little or no eye contact made when shaking hands.
- A weak handshake is not a reflection of the assertiveness of the Japanese character.
- When introduced, say "How do you do?" rather than simply "Hello", followed by your name, title and relationship to the person making the introductions.
- The exchanging of business cards (*meishi koukan*) is important business etiquette.
- Business cards (*name cards*) are very important to the Japanese. Names cards must be treated with respect. The business card carries the identity of the person.
- Print the business cards in your own language and in Japanese on the reverse side.
- Cards should be removed from a business card case (leather, plastic, or metal) and turned so that the print faces the recipient.
- Present the card using both hands accompanied by a slight bow.
- Receive a card using both hands. The card should be studied prior to bowing or shaking hands.
- Placing the card on the table in front of you is an additional sign of respect.

- Handle cards carefully. Business cards should be stored in a case and placed in the inside pocket of a suit or in a handbag.
- Never store cards in a wallet or trouser pocket.

Forms of Address

- The order of the Japanese name is family name preceded by personal name.
- When a Japanese name is translated into English, it is the decision of the individual as to the name order followed. Businessmen who deal with foreigners almost always reverse the traditional order when printing their cards in English. When in doubt, ask.
- When addressing the Japanese, use the family name with the suffix *san* (English equivalent of Mr. or Mrs.).
- Never add *san* to the end of your name. It would be considered very strange to do so.
- Alternatively, use the standard courtesy titles of Mr., Mrs., or Miss followed by the last name (do not use with *san*)
- If addressing a medical doctor or teacher (of any rank), the proper form of address is the person's last name followed by *sensei. San* would not be used in this instance.
- In some companies, professional titles are used as forms of address followed by the last name (always without *san*).
- Corporate titles and rank are very important and should be used whenever possible.
- The following is a list of titles in a typical Japanese company *(kaisah)*:

Chairman	Kaichoo
President	Shachoo
Vice-President	Fuku-shachoo
Senior managing director	Senmu Torishimariyaku
Managing Director	Joomu Torishimariyaku
Director	Torishimariyaku
General Manager of a division/Department head	Buchoo
Deputy General Manager of a Division	Fukubuchoo or Buchoo dairi
Deputy general manager of a section	Jichoo
Manager/Section chief	Kachoo
Deputy section chief	Kakarichoo or Kachoo dairi
Staff	Bu'in/Ka'in (Sha'in)
Titleless staff (slang)	Hirasha'in

- In normal daily life, regardless of how long they have known each other, Japanese will address one another by their family names.
- Do not address Japanese colleagues by their first name until invited to do so.
- Do not suggest to your Japanese hosts that you be addressed by your first name.
- Never address older Japanese people by their first name.

ENTERTAINING

- Business lunches and dinners are common. Business breakfasts are rarely scheduled.
- Most business entertaining occurs after hours in bars, restaurants, "hostess bars" (not recommended for businesswomen) or *karaoke* bars (sing-a-long bars).
- Although business entertaining is done primarily for socializing, business may be discussed.
- Expect to be entertained often.
- Wives rarely accompany their husbands to a business dinner.
- If invited to a karaoke bar, it is important to participate in the singing when it is your turn. Participation, more than singing ability, is important.
- Drinking before and during dinner is expected. Do not say "no" when offered a drink.
- In traditional restaurants and at private homes, the Japanese sit on *tatami* mats (floor mats). Men sit cross-legged and the women sit with their legs to the side.
- The Japanese rarely entertain at home. If you are invited to a Japanese home, consider it a great honour.
- Unless you are advised it will be an informal evening at home, dress quite formally. A suit and tie is suitable for a man; a dress or skirt and blouse for a woman.
- Woman should wear clothing that is suitable for sitting on a *tatami.*
- Before ringing the doorbell, it is best to remove your coat, hat, and gloves.
- Shoes must be removed before entering the home. Places shoes with the toes pointing to the front door so that they can be easily slipped on without having to turn around (otherwise it may be done by your host, which should be avoided).

- Shoes that can be easily slipped off and on (i.e. loafers and other slip-on shoes) are the preferred footwear.
- Long-handled shoehorns will be provided to assist in the putting on of shoes.
- Never wander into the kitchen of a private home.
- When using the toilet facilities, you will find a pair of "toilet slippers" for the exclusive use of this room. Leave your house slippers outside the door and slip on this special footwear. Be sure to remember to change back again before returning to the living area.
- Always reciprocate the hospitality with a gift or by inviting your Japanese colleagues to dinner.
- It is considered an honour to be invited to play golf with your Japanese colleagues.

DINING ETIQUETTE

- A disposable set of chopsticks wrapped in paper are used when dining in a restaurant or private home.
- Western utensils are only used when Western style food is served.
- Before the meal is served, a damp cloth *(oshibori)* will be distributed for cleansing the hands. The cloth should be returned to the tray after use.
- Guests with the highest ranking will be served first, followed by the eldest.
- Wait for the most important person (or honoured guest) to begin eating.
- If you are the honoured guest, you should wait until it is clear that everyone is ready to begin eating.
- Before eating, in virtually any situation, it is polite to say *Itadakimasu* (pronounced ee-tah-dah-kee-mah-soo), an expression of gratitude for what is presented and to the person who presented it. This expression is usually accompanied by a slight bow.
- Try to taste all dishes offered to you.
- When using chopsticks, with the exception of the rice, be sure to bring the food to your mouth. For rice dishes, it is proper to bring the dish towards your mouth, rather than bending over.
- Miso soup dishes should also be brought towards your mouth.
- Do not mix other foods or sauces in with the rice.
- Chopsticks, when not in use, should be left on the chopsticks rest or on the corner of your plate. Never leave them standing in a bowl of rice. This is done when the Japanese symbolically offer a bowl of rice to the dead.
- Don't pass food from one pair of chopsticks to another (associated with handing over the bones of the dead).
- Don't use chopsticks to draw a bowl closer to you.
- Don't lay your chopsticks down crossed.
- Don't pour soy sauce on your rice. Rice should remain white.
- When drinking with the Japanese, the custom is to always fill another person's cup, rather than your own. Your companion will in turn fill your cup or glass.
- When your companion is pouring, you should always lift your glass or cup from the table. Leaving either on the table is considered rude.
- The most polite way to pour is to use both hands for holding the bottle, with one underneath.
- Toasting is popular in Japan. Many toasts will be offered over the course of an evening.
- To toast, raise your drink in front of you, make eye contact, and say *Kampai!* ("drain the cup").
- It is considered polite to say to the host following a meal, *Gochisosama-deshita* (pronounced go-chee-so-sa-ma-deshi-ta). Translated this phrase means "The dishes were delicious and enjoyed".
- To get the attention of a waiter/waitress, catch his/her eye and then nod your head downward and raise your hand.
- A few days after you have visited the home, you should send a thank you note.

PUNCTUALITY

- Punctuality for business meetings is critical. Allow extra transit time when scheduling meetings in Japan due to the heavy traffic.
- For social occasions, you are expected to be punctual.

USEFUL PHRASES

Yes
Hai
(High)

No
Iie
(ee-EH)

Please
Dozo
(doh-zo)

Thank you
Arigato gozaimasu
(ah-ree-gah-too go-zai-masu)

Goodbye
Sayonara
(sigh-yoh-nah-ra)

Hello (on the telephone only)
Moshi-Moshi
(moe-she moe-shee)

Good morning
Ohayo gozaimasu
(o-high-yoh go-zigh-ee-mahss)

Good afternoon
Konnichi wa
(kon-nee-chee wah)

Good evening
Konban wa
(kon-bahn wah)

How much?
Ikura desu ka?
(Ee-koo-rah des kah?)

Cheers
Kampai
(kam-pie)

VALUES AND SOCIAL CONVENTIONS

- The Japanese believe that their culture is extremely difficult for anyone but a Japanese to understand.
- The family is viewed as the foundation of Japanese society.
- Japan is a male-dominated culture.
- There is a hierarchical nature to the social structure. This is reflected in the use of language, in seating arrangements at social gatherings, in bowing to one another and many other ways.
- The Japanese are extremely status conscious.
- Harmony (*wa*) is one of the key values of Japanese society.
- The Japanese have a keen sense of reciprocity.
- The group – family, work group, company, country – often takes precedence over the individual. A popular proverb in Japan that illustrates this point is "the nail that sticks up gets hammered down".
- Elders are revered. Be sure to show the greatest respect to the older members of the group.
- Japanese etiquette is one of the most elaborate and complex in the world.
- The Japanese will rarely say "no" outright as it is considered to be rude.
- "I will consider it", "It is difficult", or "I am not sure" may often mean no.
- Saying "no" outright may cause your Japanese colleague to "lose face".
- Do not always assume "yes" means an affirmative. "Yes" may mean "I am listening" or "Yes, I understand".
- The concept of "face" is crucial. It is important not to openly criticize or embarrass a Japanese person in front of others. A person who is embarrassed in public, shares that embarrassment with those of his group.
- Japanese can also feel embarrassment if singled out for praise.
- Modesty is considered a virtue. A foreigner should not speak about any achievements that may be perceived as self-promoting.
- Be careful not to interrupt Japanese people when they are talking.

BODY LANGUAGE

- Because Japan is a high-context culture, gestures carry a lot of meaning.
- Proper posture is very important. The belief is that spirituality is enhanced with proper physical balance. Slouching indicates a lack of balance. Maintain a square, solid posture when seated (both feet squarely on the ground, arms in the lap or on the armrests).
- If the Japanese close their eyes during a meeting or presentation, it is not due to boredom or drowsiness.
- It is considered impolite to display an open mouth.
- Older Japanese women will often cover their mouths when laughing.
- Don't blow your nose in public.

Excuse yourself and do so in the bathroom. Use a paper tissue to blow your nose, not a handkerchief.

- The Japanese often avoid sustained eye contact. To look a superior in the eyes is considered disrespectful.
- The North American "O.K." gestures (thumb and forefinger curled in an "o") means not only "O.K." but also "money" to the Japanese.
- Avoid touching, standing very close, or any prolonged physical contact with the Japanese.
- Allow for periods of silence during conversations. Silence may mean that the Japanese are thinking about an issue or something has been done to displease them. Not speaking can also convey respect for the person who has spoken or the ideas expressed. Do not try to fill in the silence with words. Allow your Japanese colleagues to speak first.
- Pointing using the index finger is considered impolite. Use the hand palm up and fingers together to point. To beckon someone, extend the arm out, palm down, and make a scratching motion towards your body.
- Japanese will often smile or laugh to disguise sadness, disappointment, anger, confusion or embarrassment. Do not automatically assume that the smile means happiness.
- When seated, it is acceptable to cross your legs at the angles or knees, but generally the Japanese consider the ankle-over-the knee cross too informal.
- It is considered poor manners to have your hands in your pockets when conversing.
- The Japanese will nod their head to show attentiveness and agreement. To indicate "no" they will either shake their head or will hold their hand in front of their face and wave it back and forth.
- A common Japanese gesture to indicate that a proposal is surprising or difficult is sucking in air quickly and audibly through the lips and teeth. It is best to try to modify your request if this reaction is received.
- To move through a crowd, the Japanese may push and shove while at the same time making repeated bows as well as karate chops in the air. This gesture means "excuse me".

CONVERSATION

- Good topics of conversation include Japanese food, arts, culture, local and country attractions, sports (particularly baseball and golf), and other countries visited.
- Avoid asking overly personal questions about a person's background or family.
- Do not discuss very personal information about yourself as it is likely to make the Japanese feel uncomfortable.
- Topics to avoid include: World War II, religion, and the minority groups in Japan.
- At business parties, do not discuss wives and families.

TIPPING

- There is no tipping in Japan.
- Workers take considerable pride in their work and may even be offended by the offer of a tip.
- International hotels and restaurants: a 10% to 15% service charge may be automatically included in the bill.
- Taxis: If the driver assists with the luggage, a tip is optional.
- Hotel maids: A small gift in an envelope can be left for particularly good service.
- Porters: A set fee will usually be posted.

DRESS & APPEARANCE

- The Japanese will form an impression from the way you dress.

Men:

- Conservative suit, shirt and tie should be worn.

Women:

- Women should dress to project a conservative image. Good quality, tailored skirt suits in dark colours with white, cream, or conservatively patterned blouses are the most appropriate. Pants are acceptable.
- Do not wear the colour red for formal business situations. It is considered too provocative.
- Do not dress in formal evening attire for dinner. A business suit is appropriate.
- Women should avoid low-cut or tight fittting clothes, too much

makeup, and elaborate costume jewellery.

- Do not wear spiked heels.
- Western style toilets are popular in Japan, but you may find squat toilets in old private houses, parks or in the rural areas. Dress appropriately.

GIFTS

- Gift giving is a significant part of social and business relationships in Japan.
- Gift giving is taken seriously. The ritual and ceremony of gift giving carries more importance than the gift itself.
- Gifts are often given at initial business meetings.
- Gifts should be presented and received using both hands accompanied by a slight bow.
- Gifts should not be opened in the presence of the giver (unless you are asked to do so).
- Allow the Japanese to present their gifts first. Follow with a gift of the same quality and value.
- Generally, for first meetings, gifts should be tasteful and moderate in price. Suitable gifts include items that reflect your country, leather goods, recorded music, books, brand name items, sporting goods, fine cognacs, or liquor. Avoid gifts with your corporate logo if it has been printed in large letters. For subsequent meetings, expensive or high quality gifts should be given. Foreign name brands are best.
- If invited to a home for dinner, it is important to always bring a gift for the hostess. Suitable gifts include: flowers, fruit, cakes, cookies, candy, or other kinds of food.
- Always have gifts wrapped in Japan. Wrapping is very important and must be done correctly.
- Never use black or black and white wrapping paper. Pastel colours are preferred. Rice paper is ideal.
- Do not give gifts in fours (associated with death) or nines (associated with hardship).

FOR WOMEN

- Because Japan is a male-dominated society, doing business in Japan will present challenges for a foreign businesswoman.
- A foreign woman is first viewed first as a foreigner, then as a woman, and treated accordingly.
- Foreign businesswomen will often feel out of place in the pubs, karaoke bars, hostess clubs, and other night spots which are designed exclusively for the entertainment of men.
- Until you have established a professional relationship, it is recommended that you decline invitations to go drinking following a dinner.
- If inviting a Japanese male to lunch or dinner, to avoid any potential embarrassment to him, be sure to invite at least one other colleague to join you.

USEFUL ADDRESSES

World Trade Center Osaka
Osaka World Trade Center Bldg.
50th Floor
1-14-6, Nanko-kita, Suminoe-ku
Osaka, 559
Japan

Fax: (81 6) 6616 4130
Tel: (81 6) 6615 7000

World Trade Center Sapporo
Sapporo International Communication Plaza Foundation
MN Building, 3rd Floor, Kita 1 Nishi 3, Chuo-ku
Sapporo 060-0001, Japan

Fax: (81 11) 219 1317
Tel: (81 11) 211 3677
Email: JDE05203@nifty.ne.jp
Website:
http://www.tokeidai.co.jp/wtcsr

World Trade Center Tokyo
World Trade Center Bldg.
Suite 3704
4-1, Hamamatsu-cho 2-chome
Minato-Ku, Tokyo 105
Japan

Fax: (81 3) 3436 4368
Tel: (81 3) 3435 5657

YOUR CULTURAL IQ

Q **When would stepping on the doorsill of a home upset the owners?**

A Buddhists believe that souls reside in doorsills. You should also avoid stepping on the doorsill of a *wat* (Buddhist temple).

Q **You have just received word that your cat has been in an accident and died. You are telling the sad story to one of your foreign business colleagues and he laughs. What is the meaning of such a response?**

A In Asia, a smile or laughter might be used to mask another emotion such as sadness, embarrassment or nervousness.

SOUTH KOREA

THE COUNTRY

Population
- 46.5 million

Capital
- Seoul (11.7 million)

Major Cities
- Pusan (4 million)
- Taegu (2.4 million)

Government
- Republic, with power centralized in a strong executive.

Climate
- Korea experiences all four seasons.
- Climate is temperate. The humidity is high.
- Spring and autumn are the most pleasant times of the year.
- Spring is mild with temperatures averaging from 10C (50F) to 13C (55F).
- Autumn has warm days and cool nights. Temperatures average between (0C) 32F and (19C) 66F.
- Monsoon season is from mid-July to mid-August. Korea receives half its rainfall during this period.
- Long and cold winters with temperatures averaging between (-9C) 16F and 3C (37F). Relatively light snowfall.

Electricity
- Both the 100 volt and 220 volt systems are found in Korea.
- Hotels usually have both levels of power.
- Electrical outlets require plugs with either two flat parallel blades or two thin round pins.

Sports
- Soccer, baseball, boxing, basketball, swimming, tae kwon do (a form of martial arts), *sirum* (a type of wrestling), mountain climbing and hiking.

Currency
- The *won* (W)

BUSINESS HOURS

Business & Government Offices
- Monday to Friday: 8:30 a.m. or 9:00 a.m. to 6:00 p.m.
- Saturday: 9:00 a.m. to 1:00 p.m.
- Employees often work past 6:00 p.m.
- Government offices close at 5:00 p.m. during the months of November to February.

Banks
- Monday to Friday: 9:30 a.m. to 4:30 p.m.
- Saturday: 9:30 a.m. to 1:30 p.m.

Stores
- Daily: 8:00 a.m. to 9:00 p.m.
- Department stores: 10:30 a.m. to 7:30 p.m. daily

HOLIDAYS & FESTIVALS

New Year's	January 1
Lunar New Year's Day	January/February*
Independence Movement Day	March 1
Buddha's Birthday	May*
Children's Day	May 5
Memorial Day	June 6
Constitution Day	July 17
Liberation Day	August 15
Chusok (Korean Thanksgiving)	September/October*
National Foundation Day	October 3
Christmas Day	December 25

*date varies

THE PEOPLE

Ethnic Groups

- 99.9% Korean with a small ethnic Chinese population.
- Korea is one of the most homogenous countries in the world.
- 72% live in urban areas (in one of the six largest cities).

Language

- Korean is the official language.
- Korean is written in *Hangu*, which has a phonetic alphabet making it easier to learn than Chinese or Japanese.
- English is widely spoken and understood. It is the language of business and is taught in school.
- Korean uses some Chinese characters along with the *Hangu* script.
- Because of its simplicity and the rather small number of letters, *Hangu* is very easy to learn even by children and foreigners.
- Throughout history, *Hangu* has been at the root of the Korean culture, helping to preserve its national identity and independence.

Religion

- Although many Koreans indicate no religious preference, the culture has been heavily influenced by Buddhism and Confucianism.
- More than 1/4 of the people believe in the folk religion called Shamanism. Not only have aspects of Shamanism been incorporated into the other religions, but elements of these religions have been incorporated into Shamanism.
- 24% of the population are Christian.
- About 25% practice Buddhism.

CONDUCTING BUSINESS

Meeting & Greeting

- Koreans will want to research your company before meeting. It is therefore important to make all appointments well in advance.
- Without a contact or reference it may be difficult to obtain an appointment.
- Try to obtain a personal introduction.
- The most opportune time for meetings is from 10:00 a.m. to 11:00 a.m. or 2:00 p.m. to 3:00 p.m.
- When entering a meeting, the highest ranking person should enter first. Others should follow according to level of importance and position.
- The traditional Korean greeting is a bow, followed by a handshake. To show respect, when shaking hands the right arm will be supported under the forearm by the left hand. Direct eye contact should be maintained.
- Foreign businesswomen will have to initiate a handshake with a Korean man.
- A Korean man will not shake hands with a Korean woman.
- Korean women generally do not shake hands and will not shake hands with a foreign man.
- At the first meeting, business cards are exchanged using both hands to give and receive.
- Be sure to have the print on the card facing the direction of the recipient.
- Have cards translated into Korean on the back.
- To show respect, business cards should be read slowly and carefully before placing them on the table in front of you.
- Business cards should be stored in a pocket above the waist. Do not put them in a back pocket.
- Never write on people's business cards while in their presence.
- Business cards are important as they establish your rank and status and will determine the amount of respect you deserve in Korean culture.
- Elderly people are respected and so should be greeted first.
- A senior person offers his or her hand first to a junior person; a junior person bows first to a senior person.
- A common greeting is *Annyong haseyo?* (Are you at peace?). To express great respect, the honorific form *"Annyong hashimnikka"* is used.
- Tea, coffee, or soft drinks are normally served prior to the start of a meeting. You should accept your cup or glass with both hands when served.
- Wait for your Korean hosts to direct you where to sit.
- Bow at the end of the meeting before leaving.
- The best periods to schedule appointments are the months of: February to June, September, November, and early December.

- Avoid scheduling appointments during vacation seasons: July, August and December.
- Business will take place at a slower pace than in North America or Europe. Be patient.

Forms of Address

- Koreans have three names. The traditional name order is the family name first (usually one syllable), followed by the generational or clan name (normally two syllables) and finally the given name.
- Many Koreans have started writing the surname last to ensure that foreigners do not address them by their first name.
- Approximately 50% of Koreans have the last name of either Kim, Lee, or Park.
- For Koreans, their identities are closely tied to their position with an organization. Therefore, when addressing a Korean, they appreciate it when their professional titles are used with the family name i.e. President Kim.
- If their position is unknown, use the courtesy titles of Mr., Mrs. or Miss and the family name. Ms. is not frequently used.
- First names are considered personal and should not be used unless invited to do so.
- Koreans will often address one another using the honorific *sonsaengnim* which means "teacher". It is used after the family name or full name.
- Married women retain their maiden name.
- In correspondence with Koreans, the correct salutation is "To my respected" followed by the title and full name. Using only the family name is inadequate.

ENTERTAINING

- Because personal relationships are critical to business in Korea, a considerable amount of time is spent in business socializing.
- Eating and drinking are often a prelude to doing business.
- Business dinners are common. Business breakfasts are rare.
- Foreign businesswomen should indicate a desire to participate in the business entertainment, as some Koreans may be hesitant in including a woman.
- Wives are seldom included in business entertainment.
- At most social gatherings, men and women will separate into two different rooms or areas to talk.
- Drinking alcohol is an important part of the business and social life of Korean men.
- Male visitors may be entertained in very expensive *kisaeng* houses or salons where women entertain men with conversation, music, and even caresses while they drink and snack.
- Traditionally, a good Korean woman would not drink, although this is starting to change among younger Koreans.
- Korean men believe that drinking is an ideal way of getting to know a person.
- It is considered impolite to refuse the offer of a drink.
- Drinking will often continue late into the night.
- At the end of a dinner or an evening of drinking, as the honoured guest you may be asked to sing. Have a simple song prepared that you can sing solo.
- A refusal will interrupt the flow of the event, whereas participating will be seen as contributing to the positive atmosphere.
- The person who extended the dinner invitation always pays the bill. Among Koreans the younger person is expected to pay for the older one.
- If invited to a home, visitors should remove their shoes before entering.

DINING ETIQUETTE

- Wait until the most honoured person (usually the eldest) takes the first bite before beginning to eat.
- The most gracious way to dine in restaurants and private homes is eating at a low table, sitting on cushions set on floors that are heated from below (*ondol* floors).
- If seated on the floor for dinner, men traditionally cross their legs. Women sit with their legs to one side. Do not sit with your legs out in front of you under the table.
- The most polite way of passing food is to use your right hand, using your left hand to support it on your forearm or wrist.
- Koreans generally do not talk a lot during meals. The food should be enjoyed without distraction. Silence is appreciated.
- Chopsticks and spoons are the usual eating utensils.

- Chopsticks should be placed on the table or the rests when finished. Leaving chopsticks on top of a bowl is considered bad luck. It is considered impolite to stick them straight up in the rice, as this is how offerings are made to ancestors.
- It is polite to refuse food twice before accepting. When Koreans are entertained, food should be offered more than three times.
- Koreans will not pour their own drink as it is traditional to fill another person's cup. Women will pour men's drinks, but will generally not pour for another woman. Be sure to raise your cup when someone is filling it to make it easier for the pourer.
- Leaving a small amount of beverage in your glass indicates that you do not want a refill.
- It is also polite to pour soy sauce into a companion's dish.
- During dinner a small communal cup is passed around for each person to drink from.
- It is considered impolite to eat any food using your fingers.
- Fruit should be picked up using toothpicks which are provided.

PUNCTUALITY

- Koreans expect foreign visitors to be punctual for business and social meetings.

USEFUL PHRASES

Yes
Ye (or) Ne
(yeh) or (nay)

No
Anio
(ah-nee-yo)

Please
Chebal
(chay-bayl

Thank you
Kamsa hamnida
(kahm-sah hamn-nee-dah)

You're welcome
Ch'onmaneyo
(chon-mahn-ah-yo)

Good morning/ Good afternoon/ Good evening
Annyong hasimnika
(Ahn-yohng hah-shim-nee-kah)

How are you?
Annyong haseyo
(Ahn-yohng hah-say-o)

Goodbye
Annyonghi kasipsiyo
(Ahn-yohng-he kaesip-si-yo)

Cheers
Konbae
(kohn-bai)

VALUES AND SOCIAL CONVENTIONS

- Korea is generally a male dominated society. Men usually have priority.
- The family forms the foundation of Korean society.
- The father is the head of the family; he and the oldest son will receive the most respect.
- When addressing an audience, Koreans will normally reverse the customary salutation by saying "Gentlemen and Ladies".
- Korean men are generally louder, more direct and aggressive than other Asians.
- Education is viewed as a very important tool for achieving professional and social success.
- The literacy rate of over 90% is one of the highest in the world.
- Education, profession, and wealth are important for determining one's social status.
- Age and seniority are respected and valued.
- *Kibun* is a vital aspect of Korean culture and affects all interpersonal relationships. It relates to mood, current feeling and state of mind. To hurt someone's *kibun* is to hurt his pride and cause loss of dignity.
- Expressions and acts of humility are central to Korean character.
- Modesty is valued.
- Establishing and maintaining harmony is very important.
- To "save face", Koreans will avoid saying "no". Koreans may say yes (even if they don't mean it) to avoid upsetting you. Ask open-ended questions that will require discussion rather than questions which will result in a direct yes or no.

BODY LANGUAGE

- Unlike other Asians, Koreans will maintain eye contact when talking. It is considered more direct and a sign of trustworthiness.
- Do not blow your nose in public.
- Pushing and bumping in public places are considered normal and acceptable practices.
- It is common to see people of the same sex holding hands or with arms around each other while walking in public. This is regarded as a sign of friendship.
- It is considered impolite to eat while walking on the street.
- Public displays of affection between the sexes are frowned upon.
- The foot is considered unclean. Avoid showing the soles of your feet (or shoes), touching anyone or moving objects with your feet. If the occasion is formal, men should keep feet flat on the floor. At other times, if men want to cross their legs, care should be taken to point soles and toes downward. It is acceptable for women to cross their legs.
- To beckon someone, extend the hand out, palm down, and make a scratching motion towards you.
- Beckoning with an index finger is considered very rude.
- Korean women generally cover their mouth when laughing. It is considered improper for them to show their teeth. This is not expected of foreign women.
- Cover your mouth when yawning or using a toothpick.
- Koreans may laugh or smile to mask embarrassment, anger or surprise.

CONVERSATION

- In getting to know you, Koreans may ask a lot of personal questions. The questions are not intended to embarrass you. You may decline answering questions you feel uncomfortable with by changing the subject or giving a humourous response.
- Good topics of conversation include sports and Korean culture.
- Koreans are proud of their heritage and country. Be careful not to voice any negative criticisms.
- Avoid discussing domestic politics, socialism, communism, spouses, and Japan.

TIPPING

- Tipping is not widespread in Korea.
- Hotels and restaurants: 10% service charge is usually included. An additional gratuity can be left for exceptional service.
- Taxis: Drivers do not expect to be tipped. It is acceptable to leave small change. You may also want to tip drivers approximately 10% if they have assisted with your luggage.
- Airport porters: Tip as per posted schedules.

DRESS & APPEARANCE

- Conservative business attire for both men and women is appropriate.
- Men should wear a suit, tie, and white shirt for business.
- Women should wear suits or dresses. Slacks are only worn for informal social occasions.
- Women should dress modestly and avoid short skirts or revealing clothes.
- Women should avoid wearing straight, tight skirts because sitting on the floor in restaurants or homes is common.
- For an evening out, men should wear dark suits with shirts and ties. Women should wear dresses.
- For casual wear, men should wear conservative slacks and shirt.
- Women should wear skirts, sweaters, and blouses. The colours yellow and pink should be avoided.
- Shorts are worn only at the beach.

GIFTS

- Gift giving is common in Korea.
- In business, it is customary to exchange gifts. Wait until the Koreans present their gift first.
- Don't give expensive gifts since your Korean contacts will feel obliged to respond with a gift of similar value.
- Use both hands to give and receive gifts.
- Wrapped gifts are never opened in the presence of the giver.
- Good business gifts include: liquor (scotch), fruit, desk accessories, impersonal products with your corporate logo on them, and arts and crafts reflective of your country.
- Clocks, although associated with death in Chinese culture, are considered to represent "good luck" in Korea.
- Do not give "four" of anything. Four is a bad luck number because of its sound in Korean.
- Gifts should be nicely wrapped in brightly coloured paper. Avoid wrappings in red or dark colours.
- When visiting a family for dinner, it is appropriate to bring a gift for the hostess such as chocolates, fruit, imported coffee, or arts and crafts reflective of your country. Liquor is inappropriate to give to a woman.

FOR WOMEN

- Korea is one of the most difficult countries in Asia for the foreign businesswoman.
- Korean men prefer to negotiate with men.
- For a woman to be successful, she must possess one or more of the following: rank, power, status, expertise or outstanding academic credentials.
- Foreign businesswomen should appear elegant, refined and very feminine.

USEFUL ADDRESSES

Korea World Trade Center
Trade Tower
159-1, Samsung-dong
Kangnam-gu, Seoul
135-729, Republic of Korea

Email: kwtcsl@kotis.net
Website: http://www.kita.or.kr

Fax: (82 2) 551 5181/5300
Tel: (82 2) 551 5163/4, 5058

KYRGYZSTAN

THE COUNTRY

Population

- 4.7 million

Capital

- Bishkek {formerly Frunze} (590,000)

Major Cities

- Osh (218,000)

Government

- Democratic republic
- The president is the head of state.
- The prime minister is the nominal head of government.

Climate

- Kyrgyzstan has a dry continental climate.
- There are four seasons.
- Summers are hot and dry. Temperatures range from 30C (86F) to 35C (95F).
- Winters are cold. Snow is common. Average temperature during this period is –18C (0F).

Electricity

- 220 volts
- Electrical outlets require plugs with two round pins.

Sports

- Soccer, wrestling, and basketball are popular.
- A number of traditional equestrian sports are enjoyed: *Aht Chabysh* (long-distance races), *up* (betting races), *Dzhorgosalysh* (wrestling on horseback), *Oodarysh* (falconry on horseback), and *Kyz Dzharysh* (girls races).

Currency

- The *COM*

BUSINESS HOURS

Business Offices and Banks

- Business, Banks, & Government Offices
- Monday to Friday: 8:00 a.m. to 5:00 p.m.

Stores

- Daily: 7:00 a.m. to 8:00 p.m.

HOLIDAYS & FESTIVALS

New Year's Day	January 1
Nooruz (New Year)	January/February*
International Women's Day	March 8
Easter	March/April*
Kurban Ait (Day of Remembrance)	April*
Orozo Ait (Ramadan feast)	*
International Workers' Day	May 1
Constitution Day	May 5
World War II Victory Day	May 9
Independence Day	August 31
Christmas (Russian Orthodox)	January 7

*date varies

THE PEOPLE

Ethnic Groups

- 52% ethnic Kyrgyz
- 21% Russian
- 13% Uzbek
- Smaller minority groups of Armenians, Byelorussians, Chinese, Kazakhs, Tajiks, and Ukrainians also exist.

Language

- The official language is Kyrgyz.
- Two major dialects are spoken (northern and southern).
- Kyrgyz is written using Cyrillic symbols, but can be transliterated with the Latin alphabet.
- Russian is the primary language spoken in urban areas.

Religion

- Islam is the official religion of Kyrgyzstan.
- The Kyrgyz are, for the most part, Sunni Muslim.
- Other religions include Russian Orthodox, other Christian religions and Judaism.
- Ancient beliefs and rituals are often combined with the formal religion.
- "Totemism" (affinity with a particular animal) is widely observed.
- Animals that are worshipped include the reindeer, white camel, snake, eagle-owl and bear.
- Shamanism is also practiced.

CONDUCTING BUSINESS

Meeting & Greeting

- The standard greeting between men and women in business is a handshake.
- Business cards are exchanged.
- It is recommended that Russian printed on the reverse side of your business card.
- The common verbal greeting is *Salamatsyzby* (Hello).
- Adult men greet with *Salaam Aleikum* (Peace be upon you). The response is *Wallaikum Assalaam* (And peace be upon you also).
- When departing, *Kosh* (Good-bye) or *Rakhmat* (Thank you) are said.
- Factory and facility tours are common at initial meetings.

Forms of Address

- The *Kyrgyz* traditional method: the person is addressed by his or her father's first name followed by *uulu* (son) or *kyzy* (daughter) and the person's own given name.
- Special titles are used for elders: *Ejay* (older sister) and *Agai* or *Baikay* (older brother). The title is used following the name.
- The Russian traditional method (which is also common): the person is addressed by the first name followed by the patrynomic (the father's given name followed by a suffix *–ovich* meaning "son of" or *–ovna* meaning "daughter of").

ENTERTAINING

- Business entertaining is usually done at the office or home.
- Entertaining at restaurants is uncommon.
- Business meetings will commonly lead to an invitation to a meal.
- Meals can often last many hours.
- Although the consumption of alcohol is prohibited by the Sunni Muslim religion, most Kyrgyz families do drink. Frequent toasting is common at meals.
- Homes range from single-family dwellings and apartments to *bohz ooi* (round tents).
- Shoes must be removed before entering a private home.
- Special slippers, called *tapochki*, will be provided.

DINING ETIQUETTE

- The most honoured guest is seated at the head of the table, facing the entrance.
- The elders will be positioned near the honoured guest.
- Seating may also be on the floor on velvet floor mats. (Seating arrangements will remain the same as for the table).
- Women should sit with their legs tucked to the side or folded under.
- Hands will be washed at the table prior to the start of the meal.
- Black or green tea *(chai)* will be served in bowls *(piallas)* at the beginning and end of the meal.
- To indicate you are finished, place your hand over the top of the bowl.

- Food is often served from a communal platter in the middle of the table.
- Drinking and toasting (using the right hand) are included in most meals.

PUNCTUALITY

- Although Kyrgyz have traditionally believed people are more important than time schedules, this is gradually changing due to the new generation of students, bankers, and merchants.
- Despite the Kyrygyz's relaxed attitude towards time, a foreign businessperson should strive to be punctual.

USEFUL PHRASES

Kyrgyz

Yes
(oo-ba)

No
(zh-ok)

Thank you
(Rukh-mat)

You are welcome
(Echnerce emes)

Hello
(Sala-matsy-zby)

Good-bye
(Kosh bolun-juzdar)

Excuse me
(Kechi-riniz)

How are you?
(Ishte-riniz kan-daj)

Good morning/afternoon
(Kut-ma-nduu kjun-ju-njuzder me-nen)

Good evening
(Kut-nam-nduu kech-in-izder me-nen)

Russian

Yes
Da
(dah)

No
Nyet
(nyet)

Thank you
Spasiba
(spa-see-ba)

You are welcome
Ne za shto
(nay za shto)

Good day
Dobriyen dyen
(doe-bree den)

Good-bye
Dosvidanya
(dos-vee-dahn-ya)

Excuse me
Izvinite
(iz-vin-eet-eh)

How are you?
Kak dela?
(kahk dee-lah)

Good morning
Dobroye utro
(doe-broy-eh oo-troe)

Good evening
Dobriy vecher
(doe-bree vay-cher)

VALUES AND SOCIAL CONVENTIONS

- Kyrgyzstan became an independent republic in 1992 after the dissolution of the Soviet Union.
- Establishing a personal relationship is essential to doing business in Kyrgyzstan. Take time to develop strong social ties.
- The Kyrgyz people can be generally characterized as hospitable, soft-spoken, tolerant, and friendly.
- Family is very important. The business, social and political network is structured along extended family lines.
- All generations show much respect to the elderly.
- Education is valued.
- Outdoor activities are popular.

BODY LANGUAGE

- Your entire hand should be used, rather than an index finger, for pointing.
- It is considered impolite to blow your nose in public.
- Public displays of affection are frowned upon.
- Avoid yawning in public.
- A gesture often used at the end of a meal by a Muslim: hands are brought together as in a prayer, at chest level, raised in a circling motion, ending at the face. This is accompanied by the word *omen*.
- Yelling is considered improper behaviour.

CONVERSATION

- The Kyrgyz people are fond of horses and sports activities related to horses.
- Other good topics include: your travels, postive aspects about the country and the arts (ballet, art, and music).

TIPPING

- There is no tradition of tipping.

DRESS & APPEARANCE

- Western-style attire is common in Kyrgyzstan.
- Foreign businessmen should wear a suit and tie.
- As this is a Muslim society, modesty in attire for women is important. Conservative business suits or a dress are appropriate.
- Kyrgyz men will wear western-style clothing. This will be worn with a traditional white wool pointed hat *(kolpak)* which is symbolic of patriotism. The highest point of the hat represents the mountains.
- In the colder months, men may wear a Russian fur hat *(tumak)*.
- Women, in the rural areas, usually wear traditional Kyrgyz clothing which consists of colourful silk dresses and head scarves.

GIFTS

- Gifts are often exchanged in business.
- Appropriate gifts include: items with your corporate logo, illustrated books, souvenirs from your home country, and alcohol.
- If invited to a home, it is appropriate to bring a gift for the hostess.
- Appropriate gifts include: candy, cake, flowers, or liquor.

FOR WOMEN

- Although business is dominated by men, Kyrgyz women are gradually entering the workforce.
- Traditional male and female roles are slowly changing.

LAOS

THE COUNTRY

Population
- 5.2 million
- 45% of the population is younger than age 15.
- Fewer than 1/5 of the residents live in urban areas.

Capital
- Vientiane (532,000)

Government
- Communist

Climate
- Tropical monsoon climate.
- Three distinct seasons. Considerable variation between areas according to latitude and elevations.
- Highest humidity experienced in March and April.
- Rainy season from May to October.
- Dry season from November to April.
- Temperatures range from 14C (57F) in January to 34C (93F) in April in Vientiane (plateau area).

Electricity
- 220 volts
- Electrical outlets require plugs with two thin round pins.

Sports
- Soccer, volleyball and basketball are popular.
- The Lao national game is *kaortorz* which is played with a rattan ball.
- Women and girls do not play sports because of the time commitment involved caring for the family needs.

Currency
- The *Kip* (Kp)

BUSINESS HOURS

Business and Government Offices
- Monday to Friday: 8:00 a.m. to 5:00 p.m.
- Daily lunch break: 12:00 noon to 2:00 p.m.
- Saturday: 8:00 a.m. to 12:00 noon

Banks
- Monday to Friday: 8:30 a.m. to 4:00 p.m.

Stores
- Monday to Friday: 8:00 a.m. to 5:00 p.m.
- Saturday: 8:00 a.m. to 12:00 noon
- Stores typically family owned. Hours may vary.

HOLIDAYS & FESTIVALS

New Year's Day....................................January 1

Chinese New Year/Tet........January/February*
Army Day..January 20
Pi Mai (Lao New Year)...............................April*
Labour Day..May 1
National Day......................................December 2

*date varies

THE PEOPLE

Ethnic Groups

- Laos is an ethnically diverse country.
- There are 68 different ethnic groups, which have been classified into three major categories based upon the relationship between altitude and habitat: *Lum*, *Theung*, and *Soung*, which indicate valley, slope, and high place.
- *Lao Lum*: Accounts for 55% of the population. Related to the Thais of Thailand, this group resides in the lowlands. Their native tongue is Lao.
- *Lao Theung*: This is the largest minority group in Lao. The *Lao Theung* are Melanesians and considered to be descendents of the earliest settlers. This group resides in the midland areas of Laos.
- *Lao Soung*: the *Lao Soung* group includes the *Hmong*, *Akha*, and *Man*. With ethnic origins in southwestern China, this group resides in the highlands and speak languages related to the Chinese or Tibeto-Burman family. Their spiritual practice is primarily animist, with influences by Chinese Buddhism and Confucianism.

Language

- The official language is Lao which is taught in the schools and is used in all official communications.
- Most Lao understand Thai because of the influence of entertainment (movies, television and radio) and trade.
- Thai, Hmong, and Lao Thung are also spoken.
- French is officially the second language, although it is no longer widely spoken. In the past, French was the language used in government and business. A small percentage of older people (over the age of 50) speak French.
- Russian is also understood by many people.
- English is spoken and because of the new western influences, may eventually become the preferred second language of Lao.

Religion

- 85% of the country practice Theravada Buddhism. It is the official religion of Laos.
- Many Laotians practice *phi* worship (animist spirits). These spirits are believed to have great influence over a person's destiny. Elements of *phi* worship have been incorporated into formal Buddhist practices.

CONDUCTING BUSINESS

Meeting & Greeting

- Between 9:00 a.m. and 11:00 a.m. is the best time to schedule meetings with Laotians.
- Try to avoid the mid-day when lunch is taken.
- The formal greeting between Laotians is the *nop* (similar to the Thai *wai*), a prayer-like gesture which involves placing both hands together at chest level. This is accompanied by a slight bow.
- To show greater respect, hands should be placed higher and higher, but never above the head.
- The most common verbal greeting is *sabadee*. The response is the same.
- The *nop* is used upon arrival and departure as well as to express thanks or regrets.
- The handshake is becoming increasingly common, particularly in the cities.
- Laotian women generally prefer the *nop* over a handshake.
- The same gesture used for greeting should be used for parting. Using a different gesture would be considered insulting.
- Before commencing business discussions, always begin with a few minutes of casual conversation.

Forms of Address

- Most Lao have just two names, their given name and their family name.
- Some older rural Lao do not possess a family name, as the custom was only adopted in 1943.
- Given names are used for most purposes. Family names are rarely used alone.
- Names are listed in the Western style with the given (first) name followed by the family name.
- Address Laotians using a courtesy title (Mr., Mrs., or Miss), professional (Dr., Professor, etc.), or official title (Police officer, President, etc.) and the first name.
- Always smile when greeting someone. For most Laotians, it is considered one of the most important expressions.

ENTERTAINING

- Most business entertaining is conducted over lunch or dinner. Breakfast meetings are rare.
- Meals are considered an opportunity to further develop relationships.
- If business is discussed, it will usually occur later in the meal.
- The meal is paid for by the person who extended the invitation.
- If invited to a home, shoes should be removed before entering unless the host indicates otherwise.

DINING ETIQUETTE

- The Lao eat with a fork in the left hand and a spoon in the right.
- Glutinous rice (a staple of the Lao diet), is eaten with the fingers.
- Most conversation takes place following the meal.
- In traditional homes, Laotians sit on mats on the floor.
- It is considered impolite to refuse any refreshments offered.
- The oldest and/or most respected person or host will take the first bite before anyone begins.
- If you are older than the host, you may be invited to take the first bite.
- Placing the lid on top of your rice basket is considered a polite way of indicating you have had enough food.
- Women should sit with legs tucked to the side. Men may sit with legs crossed or folded to one side.

PUNCTUALITY

- Try to be punctual for meetings, although delays of 5 to 10 minutes will be accepted.

USEFUL PHRASES

Yes (with respect to someone older)
Doi
(doy)

Yes (I understand)
Men leo
(men leo)

No
Bah
(bah)

Please
Kaloon/Sern
(Kaloona – as a request); (sern – as an invitation to do something)

Thank you
Khawp chye
(Khawp chy)

You are welcome
Baw pen nyang
(Baa pen nyang)

Hello
Sabay dee
(Sabay dee)

Good morning/afternoon/evening
Sabay dee
(Sabay dee)

I understand
Koi khao chye
(Khoy khao chy

No, I do not understand
Baw khoy baw khao chye
(Baa khoy baa khao chy)

Good bye
Khoy khaw la kawn
(Khoy khaw la kawn)

Toast "to good health" (don't have a standard cheer)
you dee mee heang
(yu dee mee hang)

VALUES AND SOCIAL CONVENTIONS

- Over 80% of the population are employed in agriculture.
- The Laotians are warm, frank, sincere and friendly.
- Loyalty to family and friends is important.
- The establishment and maintaining of social harmony is very important.
- Public display of strong emotions, particularly anger, irritation or disappointment, are equated with a lack of discipline (and therefore frowned upon).
- When dealing with others, Laotians believe one must always remain calm, cool, respectful, cheerful, and considerate.
- Humility, modesty, and patience are personality characteristics which are admired.
- The Lao will not usually give an outright "no" response. It is considered impolite. If there is hesitation, or any kind of excuse, or a response such as "I will try", this can be interpreted to mean "no".

- Public criticism of an individual will cause both you and the other person to lose face.
- It is considered disrespectful to openly disagree with others.
- Opinions should be expressed in a restrained manner.
- A smile may be used to disguise embarrassment, sadness or many other emotions. Do not assume it is always an expression of happiness.
- A common expression frequently used by the Lao is *"Bo pehn ngan"* which means "never mind" or "forget it" or "there's nothing to be done", depending upon the situation. Rather than get upset about situations which they may feel powerless to change, or which may potentially upset harmony and balance, the Lao will simply discount the problem by using the above expression. Life should be enjoyed at the moment.
- Every Lao village has at least one *wat*. The *wat* is either just a temple or a temple with a *sim* (a large meeting hall and dormitories housing members of the monastery) where ceremonies, festivals, and fairs are held. These events are important for the religious, social and economic life of the community.
- Traditionally, young men are expected to spend three months living and studying in a Buddhist monastery. Although this practice is not as prevalent today, men who do become novice *bonzes* (monks) are held in high esteem.
- Shoes must always be removed before entering a Lao *wat* (temple).
- No one should sit with his/her head higher than a monk. You will often see monks sitting on platforms.
- If sitting in front a Buddha image, your feet should be pointed away or tucked underneath.
- Do not touch or photograph images of the Buddha as they are considered sacred, unless you have received permission to do so.

BODY LANGUAGE

- The Lao are sensitive about the head, the hands, and the feet.
- The head is considered the most sacred part of the body. Avoid touching a person's head, even to pat the head of a child.
- Do not point using the index finger. It is considered uncouth. Use the entire hand (palm up).
- The feet are considered the least sacred. Do not use the foot to point or sit with the sole of your shoe facing a person or sacred object (i.e. Buddha statue).
- Generally, Laotians do not like to be touched. Avoid spontaneous gestures such as hugging or back slapping, unless you are good friends.
- Men and women do not show affection in public.
- Women should never touch a monk or his robe.
- Hands should be crossed, rather than held down by one's side, when conversing with a superior.
- A distance of a few feet should be maintained when conversing with a Lao in a business setting
- To beckon, hand should be outstretched, palm down, and fingers waving.

CONVERSATION

- Good general topics include positive aspects of Laos, your travels, or the weather.

TIPPING

- Although it is not customary to tip, small gestures of kindness are always appreciated.

DRESS & APPEARANCE

- The appropriate attire for men is a business suit or shirt and tie.
- Dresses, suits, or a skirt and blouse are appropriate for women.
- Although urban Lao women will wear western-style clothing, many Lao women wear western-style blouses with colourful sarong-style skirts *(phaa silz)*.
- Lao men wear casual, open-neck, short-sleeve shirts.
- T-shirts and shorts are common attire for men throughout the country.
- Formal attire for men consists of a white, long-sleeve shirt with long pants. For women, the sarong-style skirt *(phaa silz)* in silk is worn with a special blouse.

GIFTS

- Gifts are generally not required for initial business meetings.
- For subsequent meetings, although not required, gifts are appreciated and acceptable.
- If giving a gift, a moderately priced item is appropriate. A small item with the company logo or handicrafts from your home country would be suitable.
- Although you are not obliged to bring a gift when visiting a private home, small gestures are appreciated.
- Expensive gifts should be avoided as they will only embarrass your host who will feel obligated to reciprocate and may be unable to do so.
- Gifts should be accepted using both hands.
- Gifts should not be opened in the presence of the giver. To do so would imply greed or an over anxiousness to see what is inside.

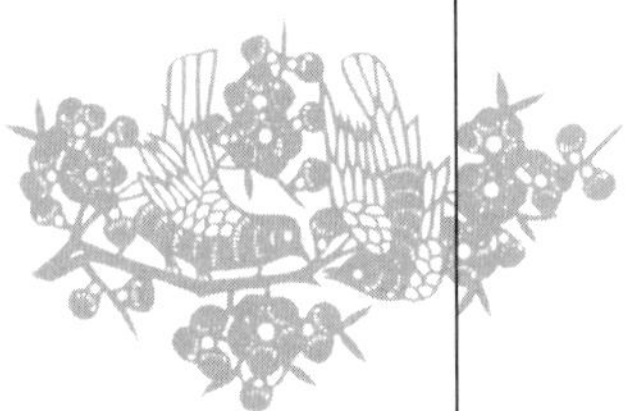

FOR WOMEN

- Although Lao is a male-dominated society, foreign businesswomen can be successful here.

YOUR CULTURAL IQ

Q **In what country would passing food with your chopsticks be frowned upon?**

A In Japan, using chopsticks to pass food is associated with "passing the bones of the dead".

Q **The western gesture to indicate "yes" is by nodding the head up and down, while shaking it back and forth indicates "no". In what country is the reverse true?**

A In Sri Lanka, nodding the head up and down signifies "no", while shaking it back and forth indicates "yes".

MALAYSIA

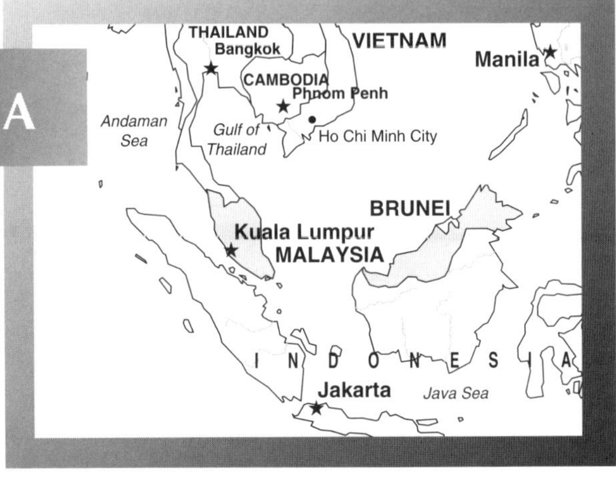

THE COUNTRY

Population
- 21.7 million
- It is a racially and culturally diverse country.
- 48% are younger than age 20.

Capital
- Kuala Lumpur (1.4 million)

Major Cities
- Ipoh (293,000)
- Georgetown (248,000)

Government
- Constitutional monarchy.
- The king is the head of state.

Climate
- Malaysia has a typically tropical climate – it is hot and humid year round (around 90% humidex). The temperature rarely drops below 21C (70 F) even at night and usually climbs to 32C (90F) or more during the day.
- Rainstorms are usually short and sharp. The monsoon season, when rainfall is more intense and temperature are slightly lower, is from mid-September to mid-December. Throughout the rest of the year, it usually rains at least once a day.
- On the east coast, and also in Sarawak and Sabah, October to February is the wet season.

Electricity
- 220 volts
- Electrical outlets vary. Plugs may be three rectangular prongs or two round short pins.

Sports
- Soccer, badminton, field hockey, cricket, rugby, and table tennis. Kite flying is popular on the peninsula.

Currency
- Malaysian dollar or *ringgit* (M$)

BUSINESS HOURS

Business Offices
- The days when business is not conducted vary according to region.
- Although a Muslim country, the Islamic workweek schedule (Saturday to Wednesday) is only followed in five Malaysian states: Perlis, Kedha, Kelantan, Terengganu and Johore.
- Generally, businesses are open Monday to Friday: 8:00 a.m. or 8:30 a.m. to 4:30 or 5:00 p.m.
- Some are open Saturday mornings: 8:00 a.m. or 8:30 a.m. to 12:30 or 1:00 p.m.
- Businesses are usually closed for one hour at lunch.
- Muslims will take a two-hour break on Fridays (if Friday is a work day) to attend a mosque.

Government Offices
- Monday to Friday: 8:30 a.m. to 4:45 p.m.

Banks
- Monday to Friday: 10:00 a.m. to 3:00 p.m.
- Saturday: 9:30 a.m. to 11:30 a.m.

In the states following the Islamic workweek:

- Saturday to Wednesday: 10:00 a.m. to 3:00 p.m.
- Some banks are open on Thursday morning.

Stores
- Monday to Saturday: 9:00 a.m. to 6:00 p.m.
- Department stores stay open until 9:00 p.m.
- Most department stores open on Sunday from 11:00 a.m. to 9:00 p.m.

HOLIDAYS & FESTIVALS

New Year's Day....January 1
City Day (in Kuala Lumpur)....February 1
Chinese New Year....January/February*
Ramadan....*
Hari Raya Puasa....March*
Labour Day....May 1
Wesak Day....May 6
Hari Raya Haji....*
King's Birthday....June 5
Awal Muharram....June 21
Prophet Muhammad's Birthday....August/September*
NationalDay....August 31
Deepavali....early November*
Christmas....December 25

*date varies

THE PEOPLE

Ethnic Groups

- 60% Malay
- 31% Chinese
- 8% Indian/Pakistani/Bangladeshi

Language

- Official language is Malay (Bahasa Melayu).
- The Chinese speak one of various Chinese dialects.
- The Indians speak Tamil.
- Numerous indigenous languages are spoken in Sabah and Sarawak.
- English, which is widely spoken and understood, is considered a unifying force.

Religion

- Islam is the official religion.
- Almost all ethnic Malays are Muslim.
- Approximately 53% of the population are Muslim.
- The Chinese are primarily Buddhists. A small percentage practice Taoism and Confucianism.
- The Indians are generally Hindu or Sikh.

CONDUCTING BUSINESS

Meeting & Greeting

- To greet a Malaysian, use a relatively soft lingering handshake. Malaysian men may use both hands to greet friends.
- Men will shake hands upon greeting and departing, both in business and socially.
- Malaysian men will normally wait for a woman to extend her hand before offering to shake it.
- Women should not offer to shake the hands of a Muslim Malay man.
- Malay women and the elderly will usually offer a verbal greeting rather than shake hands.
- It is acceptable for foreign women to simply nod and smile upon meeting a Malay man.
- The traditional greeting between Malays is the *Salaam* which involves taking the right hand, touching the heart, then the forehead and then gesturing forward. It is not recommended that foreigners use this greeting.
- When greeting an Indian man, women may wish to use the traditional greeting, *namaste*. This involves putting the hands together at chest level, as in a prayer, and bowing slightly.
- Business cards should be printed in English. You may wish to have Chinese printed on the reverse on some of your cards.
- Be sure to have the print on the card facing the direction of the recipient.
- Treat all cards with respect. After receiving a card, examine it closely before storing it away in the appropriate business card holder or inside jacket pocket. Do not store cards in a back pocket.
- Never write on a person's business card while in their presence.
- Status is important and is indicated on the business card by titles and degrees.
- Malays often use a rhetorical greeting, *"Where are you going?"*. You are not expected to provide information regarding your itinerary. One possible response is *"I am out for a walk"*.
- The Chinese rhetorical greeting, *"Have you eaten?"* should be answered with an affirmative, whether or not you have had food recently.

Forms of Address

Malays:

- There are no family names. A man is known by his given name(s) followed by *bin* (son of) and his father's name.
- A woman is known by her given name(s) followed by *binte* (daughter of) and her father's name.
- To address a Malay, use the appropriate professional title (Dr., Professor, Engineer) or Mr./Mrs./Miss followed by their given name.

- The traditional greeting for Malay men is *Encik* (pronounced onchik) followed by their first name. For a married woman it is *Puan* (pronounced poo-ahn) or for a single woman, *Cik* (pronounced chik), followed by her first name. The current trend is to use *Puan* for any adult female.
- Some married women will drop their father's name and take their husband's name.
- Some westernized Malays have removed *bin* or *binti* from their name.
- If a man has completed his pilgrimage to Mecca, he will be addressed as *Tuan Haji.* If a women has completed her pilgrimage to Mecca, she will be addressed as *Puan Hajah.* These honorific titles must be individually earned.
- Many Malays have titles such as *Dato'* or *Tan Sri* and these should be used, with or without their name following.
- *Raja* denotes a person of Royal descent. The title *Engku* is generally preferred, however, the means of address and title will vary. Ask for guidance from a native.

Chinese:

- In Chinese names, the family name is traditionally placed first, followed by the given name. Individuals should be addressed by Mr., Mrs., or Miss followed by their family name or surname.
- It is common to address the Chinese using their professional or government title followed by their surname.
- Chinese women normally keep their maiden names upon marriage. A married woman should be addressed as Madame (or Mrs.) plus her maiden family name.
- Many Chinese have taken an English first name or use their initials to ease communications with English speakers.

Indians:

- Use professional titles (Doctor, professor) or the English courtesy titles (Mr., Mrs. or Miss) plus the family name unless familiar with the Hindu, Muslim or Sikh greeting customs. Wait until invited to use first names.

Hindu:

- Given names come first, followed by family names.
- It is polite to use professional titles or *Shri* (Mr.); *Shrimati* (Mrs.) or *Kumari*(Miss) or the suffix *–ji* with a last name to show respect.

Muslims:

- Muslim Indian names follow the same pattern as Muslim Malays. Address them using the professional title or courtesy title followed by their given name.

Sikhs:

- The given name is always followed by either *Singh* (for males) or *Kaur* (for females).
- All Sikhs use the name *Singh*, but not all Singhs are Sikhs.
- Address Sikhs by their professional title or Mr., Mrs., or Miss, and by their first name.
- To address a Sikh male as Mr. Singh is the equivalent of saying "Mr. Man" in English.
- Some Malaysian Indians will use Western-style surnames. They should be addressed with their professional title or a courtesy title (Mr./Mrs./Miss) followed by their surname.

ENTERTAINING

- Entertaining visitors is an important part of conducting business in Malaysia because of the emphasis on developing personal relationships.
- Business meetings take place over lunch or dinner. Breakfast meetings are uncommon.
- Spouses may be invited to dinner, but not lunch.
- Business is not normally discussed during a meal.
- Due to the Islamic influence, alcohol is rarely consumed in restaurants. Although alcohol is served at licensed restaurants.
- Business relationships are often further established over a game of golf. Foreign businesswomen will normally not be invited to participate unless male colleagues are present.
- Most entertaining takes place in restaurants, as Malaysians do not generally invite business associates to their home.

DINING ETIQUETTE

- Malays eat with a spoon in their right hand. They may use a fork in the left hand to push food onto the spoon.
- The guest of honour is seated at the head of the table or to the right of the host.
- Take at least a small portion of any food offered. It is considered impolite to refuse.
- Do not begin eating until your hosts invites you to do so.
- Do not blow your nose or clear your throat at the dinner table. It is considered rude and should be done in private.
- There is no toasting etiquette in Malaysia.
- Hindus and Sikhs do not eat beef. Many are vegetarians.
- Muslims eat beef, but do not eat pork or shellfish.
- Orthodox Muslims and most Hindus do not consume alcohol.
- Drinks are offered and received with both hands.
- The most respectful way to hand a dish to another person is to use your right hand. The right arm should be supported at the wrist or forearm with the left hand.
- A bowl of water is usually available to wash before and after a meal.
- It is impolite to leave food on a plate.
- To beckon a waiter, use your whole hand. It is considered rude to gesture using just one finger.

PUNCTUALITY

- It is important to be punctual, although ethnic Malays may not always be on time.
- Chinese businesspeople are likely to be prompt.
- Indians will expect a visitor to be punctual, although they may not always be prompt.
- Be punctual if invited to a Malaysian home for dinner.

USEFUL PHRASES

Hello
Apa Khabar
(ah-pah kah-bahr)

Good-bye
Selamat tinggal
(she-lah-maht ting-gahl)

Yes
Ya
(yah)

No
Tidak
(tee-dahk)

Good morning
Selamat pagi
(she-lah-maht pah-ghee)

Good afternoon
Selamat petang
(she-lah-maht pet-tahng)

Good evening
Selamat malam
(she-lah-maht mah-lahm)

Please
Minta
(min-tah)

Thank you
Terimakasih
(tree-mah kay-say)

You're welcome
Sama sama
(sah-mah sah-mah)

VALUES AND SOCIAL CONVENTIONS

- It is important to always remain polite and courteous. Considerable value is placed on these attributes.
- Never raise your voice to or embarrass a Malaysian colleague.
- Malaysians are unlikely to say "no" directly.
- When Malaysians say "yes", it can be interpreted as "yes, I understand" or "maybe". It does not always indicate an affirmative.
- Malaysians respect their elders.
- Maintaining harmony within the family and community is important.
- Relationships are fundamental to doing business in Malaysia. Spend time establishing social ties.

BODY LANGUAGE

- Avoid touching someone's head (even to pat a child's head) as both Malays and Indians believe it is where the spirit or soul resides.
- There is no public contact between sexes in Malaysia, even between husband and wife.

- Kissing, even a slight peck on the cheek, is not done in public.
- It is common to see people of the same sex holding hands or with arms around each other while walking in public. This is regarded as a sign of friendship.
- For both Muslims and Hindus, the left hand is reserved for personal hygiene and therefore considered unclean. Do not eat, accept gifts, pass objects, or hold cash with your left hand. When both hands are needed, it is acceptable to use both.
- The foot is also considered unclean. Avoid showing the soles of your feet (or shoes). This includes touching anyone, moving objects with your feet, or putting them on a table whenever you are seated.
- When crossing your legs, do not place one ankle on the other knee.
- If seated on the floor, men normally sit cross-legged whereas women will sit with their legs tucked underneath them.
- Shoes must always be removed before entering a mosque.
- Do not point using your forefinger as Malaysians use this gesture to point only at animals. Use the right hand, palm facing out or your right thumb (be sure the rest of your fingers are curled inward).
- It is a sign of anger if a person stands with hands on hips.
- Avoid smacking your closed fist into the palm of your other hand as it regarded as an obscene gesture.
- The Malaysians may smile or laugh to hide embarrassment, anger or discomfort.
- Your mouth should always be covered when yawning.
- If you see a prayer mat in a Malaysian home or office, be sure to avoid stepping on it.
- An Indian may indicate agreement by a side-to-side toss of their head. Westerners often misinterpret this gesture to mean "no".
- To beckon someone, extend the arm out, hand down, and make a downward scratching motion with your fingers towards your body.

CONVERSATION

- Family, sports, food and travel are good topics of conversation. Positive comments about the country or city are also welcome.
- Avoid discussing religion.

TIPPING

- Tipping is not very common in Malaysia.
- Restaurants: There is usually a service charge on the bill. Leave only small change in addition.
- Porters: 1 ringgit per bag
- Taxi drivers: Round off the fare
- Toilet attendants: 1 ringgit

DRESS & APPEARANCE

- As a foreigner, you should dress formally until aware of the degree of informality that is accepted by the people you are visiting.
- For men, white long-sleeve shirts are considered a mark of prestige.
- The business attire for men is suit and tie; for women, a suit, dress, or blouse and skirt.
- Female visitors should dress conservatively in business situations, and will be more comfortable walking in the city if arms and legs are covered.
- For casual wear, slacks and short-sleeve shirt are appropriate for both men and women.
- Yellow is the colour reserved for royalty. Unless this colour is within a pattern, women should refrain from wearing it on formal occasions.
- Women should also avoid wearing white as it is associated with death and mourning.
- For receptions, women may wear business attire or to please their hosts, a silk *"baju kurong"*, the traditional dress of Malaysian women. Men often wear long-sleeved shirts made from the native batik material.

GIFTS

- Because of the different ethnic groups, gift giving can be complicated.
- For business, gifts are not given on the first meeting. Do not give token gifts such as corporate mementos.
- A small gift should be given if visiting a home. Fruit, chocolate or something from your native country is appropriate.
- Always give and receive gifts with both hands.
- Gifts are not opened in front of the giver.

- Do not use white wrapping paper (associated with funerals).

Chinese:

- Avoid giving clocks (associated with death) , knives (suggest the severing of relation-ships), hand-kerchiefs (symbolize grief) and white flowers (associated with mourning).
- Give gifts in even amounts.
- Do not wrap gifts in the colours of white, black or blue.

Muslims:

- Avoid giving liquor, pork items, and liquer-filled chocolates.
- As Malays consider dogs unclean, do not give toy dogs or gifts that picture dogs.

Indians:

- Items in odd numbers are considered lucky.
- Do not give gifts made of cowhide (i.e. leather picture frames). Cows are looked upon as sacred and the killing of them is equivalent to murdering a human being.
- Wrapping should be done in the lucky colours of green, red, or yellow. Avoid wrapping in the unlucky colours of black or white.
- If invited to an Indian's home for dinner it is polite to bring a small gift such as chocolates, fruit or flowers.

FOR WOMEN

- Women are generally accepted in business.
- Although women are still strongly represented in administrative and support positions, many now occupy influential roles in government and business.

USEFUL ADDRESSES

Putra World Trade Centre
Level 3, Putra World Trade Centre
41, Jalan Tun Ismail
50480 Kuala Lumpur
Malaysia

Fax: (60 3) 443 3777
Tel: (60 3) 443 3999

MYANMAR

THE COUNTRY

Population
- 46.4 million

Capital
- Yangon {Rangoon} (3.9 million)

Government
- Military

Climate
- Hot and tropical, with three seasons.
- March to June is the dry season, with temperatures between 30C (86F) and 36C (96F).
- The monsoon period, July to October, has temperatures between 29C (84F) and 31C (88F).
- November to March , considered the cool season, sees temperatures range between 31C (88F) and 33C (92F).

Electricity
- 220 volts
- Electrical outlets require a variety of plugs: two round short pins, three rectangular prongs, two flat angled blades, or three round thick pins.

Currency
- The *kyat* (K)

BUSINESS HOURS

Business & Government Offices
- Monday to Friday: 9:00 a.m. to 4:30 p.m.
- Some private companies may stay open later.

Banks
- Monday to Friday: 10:00 a.m. to 2:00 p.m.

Stores
- Open daily and for longer hours than offices. Hours vary.

HOLIDAYS & FESTIVALS

Independence Day	January 4
Union Day	February 12
Peasants Day	March 2
Tatmadaw (Armed Forces Day)	March 27
Water Festival	April*
Labour Day	May 1
Kasone Banyan (Water Festival)	May*
Beginning of Buddhist Lent	July*
Martyr's Day	July 19
End of Buddhist Lent	October*
Tazaungdaing	November*
National Day	December*
Karen New Year	December*
Christmas Day	December 25

*date varies

THE PEOPLE

Ethnic Groups
- 72% Burman (Tibeto-Chinese)
- 9% Shan
- 7% Karen
- 3% Chinese
- 2% Indian
- The other minority groups are the Kayah, Chin, Mon, and Arakanese (Rakhine). Each name refers to the region in which they live.

Language
- The official language of Myanmar is Burmese.
- It is spoken by the majority of the population.
- There are more than 80 languages spoken in Myanmar.
- English is understood and widely spoken, particularly among the elderly.
- English was forbidden under General Ne Win, so the younger generation are unlikely to speak the language.

Religion
- Theravada Buddhism is the principal religion.
- Buddhism is central to Burmese life.

CONDUCTING BUSINESS

Meeting & Greeting
- Most Burmese do not shake hands.
- A foreign businessman or woman should wait until a hand is offered, particularly with women.
- A simple nod of the head, accompanied by a smile is usually appropriate.
- The most senior person should be greeted first.
- A common rhetorical greeting is usually a question about one's health and mood. The appropriate response is a smile.
- Business cards are exchanged.
- English is the most common language used for business.
- The first meeting is often used to learn about one another and begin building a relationship.
- Meetings should begin with casual conversation.

Forms of Address
- Many Burmese have Western names, because of the colonial influence.
- Using the traditional Burmese forms of address is appreciated.
- Use the appropriate prefix with their full name.
- The prefix *U* (pronounced oo) is used as an honorific "Mr." for senior men. Use the prefix *Maung* for younger men.
- The prefix *Ma* is used for females until the age of 20.
- After the age of 20, the prefix *Daw* is used for adult women.
- Do not use first names until invited to do so.
- If confused as to the correct form of address, it is acceptable to ask is preferred.

ENTERTAINING

- Business dinner entertaining in a hotel or restaurant is common.
- Business breakfasts and lunches are rare.
- The Burmese often entertain in their homes.
- If invited to a home, you should remove your shoes before entering.
- At a private home, an offer should be made to assist with the dishes. Any effort to play with the children will be admired.

DINING ETIQUETTE

- The Burmese avoid eating pork and beef.
- The Burmese consume little alcohol.
- Seating arrangements are not important. You will likely seat yourself.
- The Burmese will often decline the offer of a second serving of food several times before accepting.

PUNCTUALITY

- Although most Burmese have a relaxed attitude towards time, foreign visitors are expected to be punctual.
- Senior government officials may keep visitors waiting for several hours.

USEFUL PHRASES

Yes
(Hote pa dae)

No
(Mahote pa boo)

Please
(Chay zoo pyu ywe)

Thank you
(Chay zoo tin ba dae)

You are welcome
(Ya ba dae)

Hello
(use the English "hello")

Good-bye
(Pyan daw mae)

Excuse me
(Khwint pyu ba)

How are you?
(Nay kaung thela?)

Good morning/afternoon/evening
(Mingala ba)

No, I do not understand
(Chundaw naa malae boo)

Cheers
(use the English "hello")

VALUES AND SOCIAL CONVENTIONS

- Relationships are critical to doing business in Myanmar. Take time to develop strong social ties.
- Personal connections are required for conducting business.
- The Burmese prefer personal contact instead of using the telephone when conducting business.
- The Burmese are uncomfortable saying an outright "no" as it causes "loss of face". A more likely negative response is "I would like to, but…".
- Do not assume "yes" means an affirmative. "Yes" can mean "Yes, I understand".
- The Burmese can be characterized as open and carefree.
- Most Burmese are respectful of astrology and will often consult a monk prior to setting a date for an important event, such as the opening of a business.
- The Burmese can also be quite superstitious.
- Families are the centre of Burmese society.
- Elders are revered.
- Excessive talk of money is considered to be in poor taste. As a result, many services and goods are provided free of charge.
- Do not assume a smile always indicates happiness. A smile will often be used to mask another emotion such as embarrassment or discomfort.
- Burmese society and its social values have been largely influenced by Buddhism.

BODY LANGUAGE

- The foot is considered unclean. Avoid showing the soles of your feet (or shoes), pointing or touching anyone using them, or moving objects with your feet.
- Do not put your feet on a chair or table. It is considered disrespectful.
- Avoid touching someone's head (even to pat a child), as the Burmese believe it is where the spirit or soul resides.
- Do not touch anyone, particularly of the opposite sex.
- Excessive displays of emotion, both anger and affection, will cause you to lose the respect of a Burman.
- Spitting is considered a gesture of contempt.
- Always show respect for Buddhist images. Do not pose for pictures in front of them unless you have received permission.
- Women are not permitted to touch a Buddhist monk.

CONVERSATION

- Appropriate topics include your travels and positive impressions of Myanmar.
- Avoid discussing politics or religion.
- The Burmese may ask questions which may be perceived as personal according to Western values. If you find any questions uncomfortable, simply be vague in your details.

TIPPING

- Tipping is not customary, although you may wish to provide an inducement to have a service performed more quickly.

DRESS & APPEARANCE

- Business attire for men is suit, long-sleeved shirt, and tie.
- Women should wear a business suit or dress. Pant suits are acceptable (although they shouldn't be worn for a first meeting).
- Women should avoid wearing the colour black at any festive events, as this is considered a sombre colour.
- The Burmese traditional dress for both men and women is a *sarong* (a wrap-around skirt), worn with a blouse (for women) or shirt (for men).

GIFTS

- A small tasteful gift should be presented at your initial business meeting.
- Appropriate gifts include: good quality pens, liquor, souvenirs from your home country, or items with your corporate logo.
- Gifts should not be opened in the presence of the giver, to avoid the appearance of being greedy.
- Most Burmese will initially refuse a gift. It is important to insist until they accept it.
- If invited to a private home, you should take a small gift such as chocolates, fruit, something small for the children or a souvenir from your home country.

FOR WOMEN

- Compared to elsewhere in Asia, women have enjoyed more freedom and equality.
- Burmese women are educated.
- Many run small family-owned businesses.

NEW ZEALAND

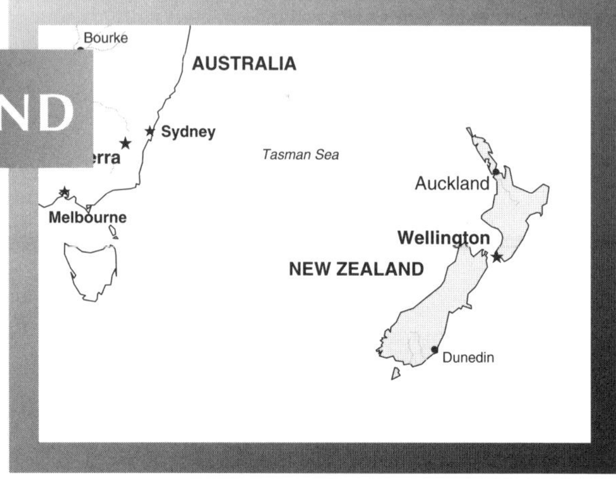

THE COUNTRY

Population
- 3.8 million

Capital
- Wellington (335,500)

Major Cities
- Auckland (997,900)
- Christchurch (331,000)

Government
- Parliamentary Democracy

Climate
- Cool, temperate climate, almost subtropical in extreme North.
- Mean temperature range, for North Island, 11C (52F) in North to 23C (74F).
- Lower temperatures in South Island.
- Highly changeable weather. All months moderately wet.
- Average daily temperature for Auckland in January is 16C (61F); in July 23C (73F).

Electricity
- 230 volts
- Outlets require plugs with two angled blades.

Sports
- Popular winter sports are rugby and soccer.
- In summer, cricket, tennis, lawnbowling, and track-and-field are favoured.
- Girls and women often play net-ball, a sport similar to basketball.
- Mountaineering, hiking (tramping), fishing (both deep-sea and fresh-water) and hunting (on a limited basis) are also enjoyed.

Currency
- New Zealand Dollar ($NZ)

BUSINESS HOURS

Business Offices
- Monday to Friday: 9:00 a.m. to 5:00 p.m.
- Saturday: 10:00 a.m. to 4:30 p.m.
- An hour is taken off at noon for lunch.

Government Offices & Banks
- Monday to Friday: 9:00 a.m. to 5:00 p.m.

Stores
- Monday to Thursday: 8:30 a.m. to 5:30 p.m.
- Friday: 8:30 a.m. to 8:30 p.m.
- On Saturday and Sunday, many shops are open.

HOLIDAYS & FESTIVALS

New Year's Day	January 1 & 2
Waitangi Day	February 6
Good Friday	March or April*
Easter Monday	March or April*
Anzac Day	April 25
Queen's Birthday	June*
Labour Day	Fourth Monday in October
Christmas	December 25
Boxing Day	December 26

*date varies

THE PEOPLE

Ethnic Groups

- 79.6% of New Zealanders are Pakeha (European descent, primarily British)
- 14.5% Maori, native people of New Zealand (Polynesian descent)
- 5.6% Pacific Islands
- 2.2% Chinese (primarily from Hong Kong) and Indians
- 1.2% Indian
- Approximately 84% of the population live in cities.

Language

- English and Maori are both official languages, although Maori is primarily used for official ceremonies and other special occasions.
- There is an ongoing effort to preserve the Maori language.

Religion

- Most New Zealanders are Christians, including Anglicans, Methodists, Protestants, Presbyterians, and Roman Catholics.
- Approximately 20% of New Zealanders have no religious affiliation.
- 1% of the population practice Hinduism or Buddhism.

CONDUCTING BUSINESS

Meeting & Greeting

- The best times to visit New Zealand for business are February to May, as well as the months of October and November. Most people are on vacation during the summer months of December and January.
- Ideally, appointments should be arranged at least three weeks in advance.
- New Zealanders are generally reserved and fairly formal upon first meet.
- Men generally shake hands when meeting and upon departure.
- The handshake should be firm and direct eye contact should be maintained.
- In formal situations, men will wait for a woman to extend her hand.
- Women will normally shake hands with other women.
- "How do you do" is the standard greeting when people first meeting.
- Once a relationship has been established, the less formal *"Gidday"* (Good-day) or "Hello" is more appropriate
- The traditional greeting among the Maori is a hug or rubbing noses (the *hongi).*
- Some Maori greeting phrases include *Naumai* (Welcome to one person), *Tenakoutou* (Welcome to many), *Haere mai* (Come hither), *Kia ora* (Hello), *Tena koe* (Hello to one person), and *Tena korua* (Hello to two people).
- When departing, Maori may say *Haere ra* (Farewell) and reply *E noho ra* (Stay well).

Forms of Address

- The order of names for New Zealanders of European descent is the first name followed by the surname (or family name).
- At first meetings, use the professional title or courtesy titles (Mr., Mrs., Miss) plus the last name.
- After initial introductions, most people will address each another by first name.
- Do not use first names until invited to do so.

ENTERTAINING

- Although initial meetings will normally take place in an office, for subsequent meetings it is customary for foreign visitors to extend an invitation to lunch at a hotel or restaurant.
- Luncheons are usually reserved for conducting business, whereas dinners are used for socializing.
- Spouses are normally included in dinner invitations.
- The main meal of the day is dinner or tea.
- *Tea* is served between 6:00 p.m. and 7:00 p.m. in homes.
- When people eat out, dinner is closer to 8:00 p.m.
- *Afternoon tea* is served between 3:00 p.m. and 4:00 p.m.
- *Supper* is a light meal or snack served in the late evening.
- In fine restaurants, waiters will normally not hurry unless requested to do so, as it is their job to let diners take their time.
- New Zealanders will often entertain at home since they enjoy cooking. Summer barbecues (*barbies*) are popular during the weekends.
- *Afternoon tea* is also popular. Substantial refreshments will be served.

- Even when not invited for a meal or *afternoon tea*, visitors will usually be served refreshments.
- It is customary for friends to make unannounced visits.
- Refreshments commonly served include coffee, tea, soft drinks, small sandwiches, cakes, and cookies.

DINING ETIQUETTE

- The continental style of eating, with the fork in the left hand and the knife remaining in the right, is used.
- Hands (but not elbows) should always be kept above the table.
- To indicate a person has finished eating, the cutlery must be placed parallel on the plate.
- Avoid speaking too loudly in restaurants. Most conversation will take place following, rather than during, the meal.
- Coffee is always served at the end of the meal.

PUNCTUALITY

- Always arrive on time for business and social events.
- Foreign visitors should arrive a little early for business appointments. New Zealanders routinely arrive five minutes early.

USEFUL PHRASES

- Although English is spoken, New Zealanders have many distinctive expressions. Some Maori words and British expressions have also been incorporated into the language.

Kiwi
A New Zealander

Pakeha
A white person

Mate or Hard Case
Friend or a humorous person

Come around
Come over

Bonnet
Hood of a car

Boot
Trunk of a car

Lift
Elevator

Bathroom
A place to take a bath (the toilet is usually in a separate room)

Company
Equivalent to North American meaning of corporation

Corporation
Equivalent to North American meaning of city or municipal government

---

A fag
Cigarette

Over the road
Across the street

Call box
Outdoor telephone booth

Kai
Food

Too right!
Definitely!

Crikey
An all purpose exclamation

Cobber
Friend

The lot
The whole thing

VALUES AND SOCIAL CONVENTIONS

- The pace of business is generally slower than it is in North America or Western Europe.
- New Zealand is an egalitarian society. A person will generally be judged by character rather than the social status and wealth.
- Consider it a compliment if someone addresses you by “mate” or “hard case” as it means they consider you either a friend or a humorous person.
- New Zealanders are friendly, hospitable, and self-reliant.
- Many New Zealanders love sports and the outdoors and are active in recreational activities such as hiking and fishing.

- New Zealand has a deep humanitarian orientation.
- The Maori and New Zealanders share many common values including truth, humility, and an emphasis on family and the community.

BODY LANGUAGE

- New Zealanders often use gestures when conversing.
- Chewing gum and using toothpicks in public are considered offensive.
- Be sure to cover the mouth when yawning or coughing.
- Ask permission before photographing anyone, particularly the Maori.
- The "V" for victory sign is considered obscene if the palm is turned inward.
- During conversation, avoid standing too close to a New Zealander. Personal space is usually important.

CONVERSATION

- Avoid making comparisons with or praising Australia. A strong rivalry exists between the two countries.
- Do not discuss religion or racial issues, especially with respect to the treatment of the Maori.
- Good topics of conversation include sports, the weather (since it is often so pleasant), their homes and gardens. Gardening is one of the most popular leisure activities.
- New Zealanders are proud of their country. Good topics therefore include positive aspects about the country or local region and culture.
- Leisure activities and family interests are often discussed.
- Political discussions are popular. Be prepared to participate and debate without causing insult.
- Having some background information on New Zealand's nuclear-free policy is useful.

TIPPING

- Tipping is generally not expected, as most New Zealanders believe that adequate compensation is the responsibility of the employer rather than the customer.

DRESS & APPEARANCE

- Business dress is conservative and quite formal.
- Men should wear a dark suit and tie.
- A dress or skirt suit and blouse are suitable attire for businesswomen.
- Because of the temperate climate, warm clothes and rain gear are required most of the year.
- The general attire is quite casual.
- Shorts are generally reserved for recreational activities.

GIFTS

- When visiting a private home for dinner, guests almost always bring a gift.
- Good gifts include wine, flowers, a potted plant, or a box of chocolates.
- Gifts that might be considered ostentatious should be avoided.

FOR WOMEN

- Although New Zealand women are still fighting for equality in wages and influence, New Zealand does not present any substantial barriers to the foreign woman wanting to do business here.

USEFUL ADDRESSES

World Trade Centre Auckland
100 Mayoral Drive
P.O. Box 47
Auckland, New Zealand

Fax: (64 9) 309 0081
Tel: (64 9) 309 6100
Email: wtc@chamber.co.nz

PAKISTAN

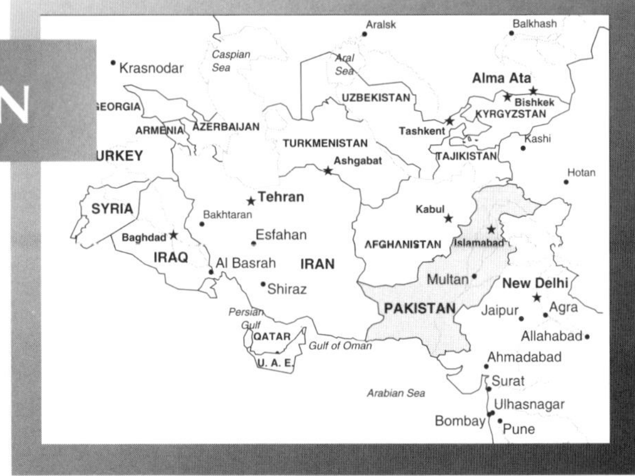

THE COUNTRY

Population
- 135 million
- 10th most populated country in the world.
- More than 40% of the inhabitants are younger than age 15.
- 67% live in rural areas.

Capital
- Islamabad

Major Cities
- Karachi (9.7 million)
- Lahore (5 million)
- Faisalabad (1.8 million)

Government
- Parliamentary democracy in a federal setting.

Climate
- Continental with many temperature variations.
- Dominated by the Asiatic monsoon.
- Pakistan has very hot summers and relatively cold winters (severe winters in the mountainous regions).
- In the summer months, from March until June, temperatures can reach as high as 45C (113F).
- In the winter months, from October to February, temperatures can dip to below freezing.
- The monsoon season brings heavy rains and hot temperatures during the period of July to October.

Electricity
- 220 volts
- Electrical outlets require plugs with either two thin round pins or three round prongs.

Sports
- Field hockey, cricket, squash, soccer, *"kabaddi"* (a type of team wrestling), polo and tennis are popular sports.
- Pakistanis are world-class competitors in field hockey and squash.

Currency
- The *rupee* (Rs)

BUSINESS HOURS

Business Offices
- Sunday to Thursday: 9:00 a.m. to 5:00 p.m.
- Closed for one hour at 1:00 p.m. for lunch.
- Saturday: Some offices will be open in the morning. Hours vary.

Government Offices
- Saturday to Thursday: 8:00 a.m. to 2:30 p.m. or 3:00 p.m.

Banks
- Sunday to Thursday: 9:00 a.m. to 1:00 p.m.
- Saturday: 9:00 a.m. to 11:30 a.m. or 12:00 noon

Stores
- Daily, except Friday: 9:00 a.m. or 10:00 a.m. to 6:00 p.m. or 7:00 p.m.

- All offices, banks, and stores are closed on Fridays, the Muslim Sabbath.

HOLIDAYS & FESTIVALS

Ramadan....January/February*
Eid-ul-Fitr
(end of Ramadan)....February/March*
Pakistan Day....March 23
Good Friday/Easter....March/April*
International Labour Day....May 1
Eid-ul-Azha (Feast of Sacrifice)....May/June*
Ashura....June/July*
Bank Holiday....July 1
Muharram....July/August*
Eid-Milad-un-Nabi (the Prophet
Mohammed's Birthday)....August*
Independence Day....August 14
Defense of Pakistan Day....September 6
Death Anniversary of
Mohammed....September 11
Iqbal Day....November 9
Birthday of Mohammed
Ali Jinnah....December 25
Bank Holiday....December 31

*date varies

- Avoid scheduling trips during major Muslim holidays, such as Ramadan, and during the Monsoon season.

THE PEOPLE

Ethnic Groups

- There are five major ethnic groups in Pakistan: Punjabi, Sindhi, Baluchi, Pashtuns (also called Pathans), and Mahajir (Muslim immigrants from India and their descendants).
- More than 3 million Afghan refugees are living in camps along the border.
- There are also numerous smaller ethnic groups.
- The largest ethnic group are the Punjabi, representing 65% of the population.

Language

- Urdu and English are the official languages of Pakistan.
- Although only 7% of the population speak Urdu as a native tongue, most people in the country speak it in addition to their own language.
- Urdu was adopted because it was the language of the Muslim Moghul Empire.
- Urdu is being encouraged as a replacement for English.
- English is used by the educated elite.
- English is commonly used in business and the government.
- Each province is free to use its own regional languages and dialects (such as Punjabi, Sindhi, Baluchi, and Pashtu).

Religion

- 97% of the population are Muslims.
- Most of these (77%) are Sunni Muslims.
- The remainder are Shiite (*Shi'a*) Muslims.
- There are over 70 Islamic sects; most fall under the Sunni and Shiite.
- Religion serves as a unifying force amongst the diverse ethnic divisions.
- 2% practice Hinduism.
- 1% are Christians (mostly descendants of mainly low-caste Hindu converts) or adherents of other religions.
- Freedom of worship is guaranteed.
- Pakistani Muslim men pray five times a day.
- Islam pervades every aspect of daily life.
- Muslims believe their fate is subject to the will of *Allah* (God).

CONDUCTING BUSINESS

Meeting & Greeting

- Pakistani men usually greet each other with a handshake, although close friends may embrace if meeting after a long time.
- Most men will shake hands with a foreign businesswoman.
- Very traditional Muslim men will avoid touching a woman.
- Wait for a Pakistani woman to offer her hand.
- Pakistani women normally do not shake hands with other women. Women usually greet one another with a hug. However, Pakistani women in senior management positions will likely be aware of western business practices.
- Verbal greetings may include questions about one's health and family. These inquiries may take some time.
- The most common Pakistani greeting is *Assalaam alaikum* (May peace be upon you).
- The reply is *Waalaikum assalaam* (And peace also upon you).
- Greet the most senior person first.
- Business cards are exchanged.
- Pakistanis are impressed by titles. Be sure these are indicated on your business card.
- Take time to socialize and build rapport before beginning serious business discussions.
- Tea or some other beverage will normally be served. It is considered impolite to refuse.

- Handshakes are used at the end of a meeting, before departing.
- The best time to schedule appointments is between 10:00a.m. and 1:00 p.m.
- Contact should be made at least a month in advance for appointments.
- Appointments should be made at least a week in advance if staying in Pakistan.

Forms of Address

- Pakistani names are complex and can be confusing.
- There will usually be three names. The surname can appear at the beginning or end of the name.
- Sometimes the name at the end may be a noble or high-ranking title.
- Occasionally the first name is the caste name and would not be used in normal address.
- It is best to ask how a Pakistani would prefer to be addressed.
- Address Pakistanis using the courtesy titles (Mr. or Mrs.) followed by the surname. Or, alternatively, use an academic or professional title followed by the surname.
- The Pakistani equivalent of "Mr." is *sahib*; for women, it is *begum*. These titles follow the surname. *Sahib* and *begum* can also be used after the professional title (i.e. Doctor Sahib).
- As the name of the Prophet is "Mohammed", it is inappropriate to address a man with just this name.
- Do not address Pakistanis by their first name until invited to do so.

ENTERTAINING

- Most business entertaining takes place over dinner, rather than lunch. Breakfasts meetings are rare.
- As the primary purpose of a dinner meeting is for socializing and developing relationships, business is not normally discussed.
- Socializing will occur prior to the commencement of eating. One should leave soon after the meal is finished.
- Spouses are not usually invited to a business dinner.
- It is important to reciprocate by inviting your Pakistani colleagues to lunch or dinner.
- In traditional homes, men and women do not socialize together. Refreshments will be served to men in a special room.
- In large groups, men and women eat in separate areas.
- If entertained in a home, dinner will normally be served very late in the evening (as late as 11:00 p.m.).
- Be sure to remove your shoes before entering a Pakistani home.
- Pakistanis are extremely hospitable and will endeavour to ensure guests feel welcome and have plenty to eat.
- During the month of *Ramadan*, Muslims will not eat or drink from sunrise to sundown each day.
- During *Ramadan*, foreign visitors, as a polite gesture, should not eat or drink in front of Muslims during daylight hours.

DINING ETIQUETTE

- Muslim Pakistanis do not consume alcohol or eat pork.
- Never use your left hand for eating or passing food. The left hand is used for bodily hygiene and is considered unclean.
- In urban areas, people may eat with utensils or their hands.
- *Chapati* (bread) is used for scooping up food when hands are used for eating.
- A spoon and fork are the utensils used. The spoon is held in the right hand, with the fork positioned in the left to push food onto the spoon.

PUNCTUALITY

- Although Pakistanis are often late for business meetings, they expect their foreign visitors to be punctual.
- For social occasions, guests will normally arrive 15 to 60 minutes late.
- Pakistanis have a relaxed attitude towards time. This is reflected by the Urdu word *"kal"* which translates as both "yesterday" and "tomorrow".

USEFUL PHRASES

Hello (Peace be upon you)
Salam Alikum
(Sah-laam a-lie-come)

Response to hello (And peace be upon you also)
Vaalaikum Salaam
(vah-lie-com-sah-laam)

Please
(Meherbani kar kay)

Thank you
(Shukriya)

You are welcome
(Sah-laam a-lie-come)

How are you?
(Kya hall hai)

God be willing
(Inshallah)

I understand
(Mein samaj gaya – male)
(gai-ee – female)

No, I do not understand
(Mein nahin samja)

Good bye
(Khuda hafiz)

Excuse me (polite)
(Maaf-ki-ji-yeey)

VALUES AND SOCIAL CONVENTIONS

- In 1991, the government declared the Koran – the holy book of Islam – as the basis of all civil law.
- Western legal and business practices also exist resulting in a mixed system that is opposed by some Pakistanis.
- The family is the foundation of Pakistani society. The male leader is the decision maker.
- Pakistanis are very class-conscious due to the past influence of Hinduism.
- Pakistan is a nation of diversity. Differences exist between ethnic groups as well as rural versus urban dwellers.
- Considerable respect is given to elders.
- Pakistanis are quite serious and formal when conducting business. Do not tell jokes in a formal business environment.
- Following British tradition, driving is done on the left-hand side of the road.
- Although it is not common, Islamic law permits a man to have up to four wives.
- Do not assume that "yes" indicates an affirmative. "Yes" can simply mean "Yes, I understand" rather than "Yes, I agree".
- Pakistanis are uncomfortable saying "no" outright. Try to avoid asking questions which require a yes/no response.
- Do not lose your temper. Greater respect will be earned for patience.
- Men and women do not generally socialize together.
- The direction of Mecca is indicated in every hotel room.

BODY LANGUAGE

- Never let your foot or shoe point at another person. The sole of the shoe is considered dirty.
- When crossing the legs, be careful to position the feet so they do not point directly at others.
- Women should never wink.
- Shoes must be removed before entering a mosque.
- To beckon a person, extend the hand out, palm down, and make a scratching motion towards the body.
- To gesture with a closed fist is considered obscene.
- The Muslim practice of praying five times per day is strictly observed in Pakistan. Never interrupt someone praying.
- Do not photograph Pakistani women without receiving permission first.
- Two men may be seen holding hands while walking in public. This is regarded as a sign of friendship.
- Do not use individual fingers to make gestures. It is considered impolite.
- Members of the opposite sex do not touch one another in public.
- Items should be passed with the right hand, or both hands.

CONVERSATION

- Good topics of conversation include: sports, positive remarks about Pakistan, your travels, the weather and general questions about someone's family and children. Unless you know an individual well, it is not acceptable to ask about his wife.
- Topics to avoid include: religion, local politics, the standard of living, comparisons with India, Israel and Jews.

TIPPING

- Tipping is expected and appreciated in the urban areas of Pakistan.
- In rural areas, tips may be returned as hospitality is considered an Islamic obligation.
- Major hotels and restaurants: 10% is expected.

DRESS & APPEARANCE

- Because Pakistan is an Islamic country, attire should be modest and conservative.
- For business, men should wear a suit and tie.
- Women should keep their arms covered. Avoid short skirts and clothes that accentuate the figure.
- Longer skirts and dresses or dressy pants with a short-sleeved blouse are appropriate attire.
- Dark suits (no tuxedos) are expected for formal events; women should wear a street length dress or skirt.
- Shorts are worn by men only for athletic events. They are never worn by women.
- Jeans are acceptable for both sexes.
- The national dress for the Pakistani is the *shalwar-qameez* (two-piece pantsuit). It is made of cotton and worn by both men and women.
- For men, solid, plain colours are worn. A vest or coat may be added for formal occasions.
- Women will wear brighter colours and bolder patterns.
- Women will wear a *dupatta* (scarf) around their heads and sometimes another long scarf around their shoulders.
- Men will usually wear some kind of headdress. It is often possible to determine a man's ethnic group from his headwear. Some wear turbans, others pillbox-type hats, and others *karakuli* (fez-type) hats. There are many variations.
- Despite the heat, Pakistanis cover their heads, arms, and legs in public.

GIFTS

- Although you are not obliged to bring a gift, small gifts are always appreciated and will earn you goodwill.
- Suitable business gifts include: pens, Swiss knives, watches, transistor radios, and items with company logos.
- A gift will politely be refused two or three times before being accepted by a Pakistani.
- Foreign visitors should follow the same pattern of refusal before accepting a gift.
- When invited to a private home, a small gift is appropriate. Dried fruit, candy, chocolates, or flowers are welcomed. Do not give alcohol unless you are aware that your hosts drink it.

FOR WOMEN

- Foreign businesswomen will experience considerable difficulty conducting business in Pakistan.
- Businesswomen will need to establish a sponsor prior to arrival. The sponsor should assist in making all the necessary arrangements, including providing a car and driver.
- It will be difficult for a foreign businesswoman to pay for a meal when entertaining a Pakistani man. Arrangements for payment of the bill should be made prior to the meal, or alternatively, entertaining can be done at the hotel restaurant with the meal being charged to the room.
- To obtain service in a bank or post office, women will need to be aggressive or men will be waited on first.
- Some Pakistani women observe purdah. A practice among Muslims and some Hindus, it means that the woman is kept in seclusion and out of sight of all men (except the family).
- Although Pakistani women are considered inferior to men, the status of women in cities is gradually improving. Women are excelling in professions.
- There are no formal restrictions on women's activities, such as driving a car.

YOUR CULTURAL IQ

Q **What country has been called the "Land of Smiles".**

A Thailand has been called the "Land of Smiles" as the Thais smile most of the time. The Thai people can be characterized as easy-going, fun-loving, pleasant, patient and hospitable. Foreign visitors should smile often.

Q **You are visiting the home of your Malaysian friend and decide to bring a small gift of a toy dog for their child. You later discover that your friend was not pleased with the gift and stored it away. Why?**

A Malays consider dogs unclean. It is therefore inappropriate to give toy dogs or gifts that picture dogs.

PHILIPPINES

THE COUNTRY

Population
- 68 million
- It is a young population, 50% of the people are below 22 years old.

Capital
- Manila (8.6 million) (Located on island of Luzon)

Major Cities
- Quezon (1.7 million)

Government
- Republic since 1946

Climate
- Tropical. Cool dry season from December to February. Temperatures 21 C (70F) to 31 C (88F).
- Hot summer season from March to May. Temperatures 22C (72F) to 34C (93F).
- Monsoon and typhoon season, June to November. Temperatures 24C (75F) to 33C (91F).

Electricity
- Most residents and business centers in the Philippines use 220 volts.
- A number of hotels also have 110 volts.
- Electrical outlets require plugs with either two thin round pins, or two flat parallel blades.

Sports
- Basketball, baseball, softball, soccer, tennis, horse racing and cockfighting.

Currency
- Philippine peso (P) = 100 centavos

BUSINESS HOURS

Business Offices
- Monday to Friday: 8:00 a.m. to 5:00 p.m.
- Offices often close for lunch from 12:00 noon to 1:00 p.m. (or as late as 2:00 p.m.)
- Some offices are open on Saturdays from 8:00 a.m. to 12:00 noon
- Many business people still be contacted after hours.

Government Offices
- Monday to Friday: 8:00 a.m. to 5:00 p.m.
- Government officials will only accept calls at the office (see Conducting Business section).

Department Stores
- Daily: 10:00 a.m. to 8:00 p.m.

HOLIDAYS & FESTIVALS

New Year's Day (Bagong Taon)........January 1
Maundy Thursday
(Huwebes Santo).........Thursday before Easter
Good Friday
(Viyernes Santo).............Friday before Easter*
Easter (Pasko ng
Pagkabuhay)......................................March/April
Bataan and Corregidor Day (also known as
Heroism Day)..April 9
Labour Day...May 1
Independence Day ....June 12
National Heroes Day.....Last Sunday of August
All Saints' Day
(Todos los Santos)...........................November 1
Bonifacio Day................................November 30
Christmas Day (Pasko)................December 25
Rizal Day...December 30
Last day of the year.....................December 31

*date varies

THE PEOPLE

Ethnic Groups

- Majority of the population is of Malay origin: Christian Malay 91.5%; Muslim Malay 4%; Chinese 1.5%; Other 3%.
- However, the roots of many of its traditions, practices and cuisine preferences are not only Malay but also Spanish, American, Chinese, and Islamic.
- People from the Philippines are called *Filipino* (male) or *Filipina* (female).

Language

- There are over 100 regional dialects spoken in the country.
- Pilipino (based on Tagalog) is the national language, although English is widely spoken and extensively used in business, government, and education. Spanish is another popular language.
- It is considered rude to speak in a dialect when someone is present who may not understand.

Religion

- Predominantly Roman Catholic (83%)
- Protestant (9%)
- Muslim (5%), practiced by the Moros who live mainly on the southern islands of Mindanas
- Buddhist and other (3%)

CONDUCTING BUSINESS

Meeting & Greeting

- Greetings are friendly and informal.
- The customary greeting is a handshake and a big warm smile.
- Respect is shown for elders by greeting the oldest person first.
- For foreign businessmen to male colleagues, handshakes are generally firm and offered during all introductions and departures.
- Men should wait for the woman to offer her hand.
- It is acceptable for a foreign businesswoman to extend her hand to both Filipino men and women.
- A common greeting between Filipinos is a slight nod of the head and a slight raising of the eyebrows, along with a friendly smile.
- Filipinos are generally more physical then other Asians and may pat one another on the back. It is not recommended that a foreigner initiate the gesture.
- It is considered a sign of respect when children take an individual's hand and press it against their forehead.
- Business cards are exchanged. Cards printed in English are acceptable.
- The exchange of cards is a less formal practice compared to other Asian countries. Your card should be offered first.
- If you are offered a card with a Filipino's home telephone number on it, it is an invitation to call.
- Socializing outside of the office is an important component to succeeding in business here.

Forms of Address

- Because of 300 years of Spanish rule, most Filipino families have a Hispanic name.
- Authority is respected. Titles and positions impress Filipinos.
- Address individuals by their professional title and surname.
- Alternatively, individuals can be addressed by their title preceded by Mr., Mrs. or Miss. Example: Mr. Attorney.
- Professors and doctors should be addressed appropriately.
- The professions where the title will always be used in both formal and informal conversation and in correspondence include attorneys, engineers, doctors, and professors.
- When a professional title is unknown or not applicable, the individual should be addressed as Mr., Mrs., or Miss. You should continue to use titles until otherwise advised.
- Although Filipinos commonly use first names, do not use them until you are invited. The exception is with very senior people in rank or age. Formality is required. "Sir" or "Ma'am" or the individual's title followed by last name should always be used.
- The wives of individuals with important positions are often addressed as "Mrs. followed by the husband's title". Example: Mrs. Mayor.
- If a woman is "widowed", the word *"vda"* will appear between her maiden name and her husband's family name.
- A *Minister* is a religious official, not a government official. Government ministers are called *Secretaries* and should be properly addressed as *Mr. Secretary.*
- In social correspondence, *Sincerely* is often used, whereas *"Respectfully yours"* is considered a complimentary form for business letters.

ENTERTAINING

- Business is often conducted at meals.
- Business breakfasts are common.
- Lunches are considered casual business meetings.
- Dinner meetings are more formal and normally conducted when relationships are more developed.
- It is socially acceptable to be late for a business dinner.
- Foreigners may expect their Filipino conterparts to arrive 20 to 30 minutes late.
- After finalizing a business deal, it is considered courteous to invite your Filipino colleagues to dinner at a restaurant. As the host you should be punctual.
- When extending dinner invitations, it is important to repeat your invitation by phoning and reminding, otherwise the invitation will not be taken seriously.
- Being entertained at a Filipino home is common once a relationship has been established.
- If you are invited to a Filipino home, arriving around 15 minutes after the appointed hour is considered acceptable as this gives the host ample time for last minute checks.

DINING ETIQUETTE

- Trying the local cuisine will endear you to Filipinos, as food is an important part of their culture.
- Food is generally served all at once, rather than in courses.
- Place settings will consist of a fork and spoon. You may find a knife in some homes.
- To eat with a fork and spoon, the fork should be used in your left hand to maneuver food onto the spoon.
- Keep your hands above the table during dinner.
- Utensils should be placed horizontally on your plate, when finished.

PUNCTUALITY

- Foreigners should be punctual for business meetings.
- Filipinos are generally on time for appointments.
- It is acceptable to be a little late (up to 20 minutes) for social events.

USEFUL PHRASES

Hello
Kumusta
(kuh-moos-tah)

Good Morning
Magandang umaga
(Mah-ghan-dang oo-maga)

Good Afternoon
Magandang hapon
(Mah-ghan-dang hah-pon)

Good Evening
Magandang gabi
(Mah-ghan-dang ga-bee)

Please
Paki
(Pa-kee)

Thank you
Salamat
(Sah-lah-maht)

Good Bye
Paalam na po
(Pa-ah-lam nah poh)

You are welcome
Walang anuman
(Wah-lahng ah-noo-mahn)

Yes
Oo
(Aw aw)

No
Hindi
(Hin-dee)

Excuse me
Ipagpaumanhin
(Eepahk-pawman-hin)

VALUES AND SOCIAL CONVENTIONS

- Education is valued. The literacy rate is approximately 90 percent.
- Filipinos are *present oriented* and therefore tend to live "in the moment".
- They are relaxed, casual, spontaneous and hospitable people.
- The family is the central unit. Members feel a great sense of obligation and loyalty to one another.
- Filipinos smile often and in various emotional situations. A smile, however, may not always be to convey happiness. It may be used to disguise discomfort, sadness, or nervousness. For example, a Filipino may smile or laugh as he describes the illness of a family member.

- Smiles are an important part of the culture and foreigners are encouraged to do it often.
- Social harmony is central to Filipino culture.
- *Amor propio* and *pakikisama* are two words used to express harmony. *Amor propio* translates as "harmony" and relates to self-respect. *Pakikisama* refers to smooth interpersonal relations.
- It is important to avoid expressing anger in public. Confrontation should be avoided.
- Be careful to avoid openly criticizing a Filipino as the negative remarks may affect his social standing.
- Being overly direct or blunt is considered uncouth.
- Because conflict is avoided, a Filipino finds it difficult to say "no". They are likely to say "yes" which can mean anything from "yes, I understand" to "perhaps" to "I hope you can tell that I actually mean no".
- A quiet gentle tone of voice should be used at all times.
- You will be asked many personal questions. Filipinos feel that they must get to know you and will want to hear about your personal background and family. It is acceptable to respond with similar questions, particularly regarding the family.
- Ask permission before photographing anyone.
- Show respect for the elderly. Be sure to greet them first.
- Younger people will normally seek guidance from elders within the family and in daily interactions in school, work and social life.
- It is important to share food with those around you.
- A Filipino may refuse a verbal invitation two or three times before accepting.
- Filipinos are meticulous about personal hygiene and are especially sensitive towards smells.
- Drinking alcohol to excess is considered rude.

BODY LANGUAGE

- Extending the middle finger and using it to point at a person is considered the most obscene gesture in the Philippines.
- Since pointing with fingers may be mistaken for a rude gesture, Filipinos will use a glance or purse their lips and point with their mouth.
- Staring, or long periods of eye contact, is considered rude.
- Avoid standing with your hands on your hips as this is considered an aggressive stance and may be interpreted as a challenge.
- To beckon someone, you should extend your hand out, palm down, and make a scratching motion towards your body.
- To indicate "two" with fingers, you should raise your ring and pinkie fingers. The thumb is not used for counting numbers.
- When walking through a crowd, or passing in front of people, a Filipino may stoop and make a "chopping" motion with the hand.

CONVERSATION

- Good topics to discuss include culture, history and business.
- Filipinos are very family oriented and will therefore enjoy discussions about their family as well as yours.
- Topics to avoid include politics, religion, local conditions and corruption and foreign aid.

TIPPING

- Tipping is common and expected.
- Attempt to carry some small bills at all times as they may be difficult to obtain outside the larger cities.
- Moderately priced restaurants: leave a small tip even if a service charge has been included.
- Expensive restaurants: 15% of the total bill should be left as a tip.
- Porters, barbers, doormen, and beauticians: leave a small tip.
- Taxi drivers: 10% of fare rounded to nearest P5 or P10.
- U.S. currency is accepted and appreciated.

DRESS & APPEARANCE

- Dressing correctly is important to Filipinos as it is considered reflective of status and authority.
- For men, suits are appropriate for business situations.
- For women, suits and dresses in bright colours are more appropriate than dark sombre colours.
- Women should not wear pants for business meetings.
- The Philippines are less conservative than neighbouring countries. Shorter skirts and sleeves are acceptable here.
- Local businessmen will wear a barong taglog, a traditional embroidered open-necked shirt worn outside the trousers.
- For casual wear, men can wear open-collar shirts and pants.
- For women, slacks or jeans are acceptable.
- Shorts and sandals, for both men and women, should only be worn when at the beach or pool.

GIFTS

- If invited to a home, it is appropriate to bring flowers, a cake, fruit, candy or chocolates.
- Thank you notes are appreciated.
- After a dinner party, it is customary for Filipinos to give guests the extra food to take home.
- Gifts are not opened in the presence of the giver.

FOR WOMEN

- Foreign women will not have problems doing business in the Philippines.
- Women are active in both government and the corporate world.
- Filipino women rarely, if ever, smoke in public.
- It will embarrass a Filipino male, if a foreign woman tries to pay the restaurant bill.

USEFUL ADDRESSES

World Trade Center Metro Manila
WTCMM Complex, Financial Center Area
Roxas Blvd., along Sen. Gil Puyat Ave. Ext
Pasay City, Philippines 1300

Fax: (63 2) 551 52535243
Tel: (63 2) 551 5151
Email:
worldtradectrmaila@netasia.net

YOUR CULTURAL IQ

Q **The order of a person's name in Western culture is first the "given name", followed by "family name". In what culture is the reverse order true?**

A In Chinese culture, the family name comes first, followed by the given name. In business, address the Chinese using the appropriate English courtesy title (Mr., Mrs., or Miss) or professional title and the family name.

Q **In what culture would the gift of a clock be considered inappropriate?**

A In Chinese culture, a clock is associated with death. Watches are acceptable.

Republic of SINGAPORE

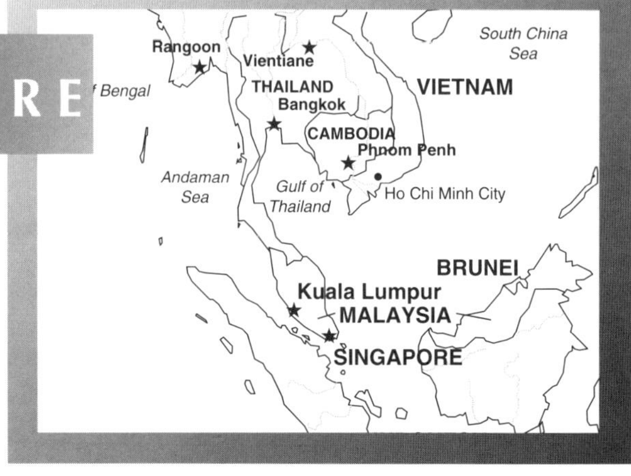

THE COUNTRY

Population

- 3.5 million

One of the most densely populated countries in the world.

Capital

- Singapore (3.3 million)

Government

- Singapore is a democratic republic.
- The president is the head of state.
- The prime minister is the head of government.

Climate

- Singapore is located just north of the equator; consequently the weather is hot and humid year all year around.
- A tropical rain shower occurs every day or two throughout the year except during the month of July.
- Mid-November to mid-January is the heavy rainy season.
- The coolest period is during the months of December and January. Temperatures range from 25C (75F) to 28C (82F).
- Temperatures during the rest of the year range from 27C (81F) to 31C (88F).

Electricity

- 230 volts
- Most hotels have transformers for 110 and 120 volts.
- Electrical outlets require four possible plug configurations: two round thick pins, three rectangular prongs, two thin round pins, or three round prongs.

Sports

- Soccer, badminton, basketball, tennis, golf, and all kinds of water sports are popular.

Currency

- The *Singapore Dollar* (S$)

BUSINESS HOURS

Business Offices

- Monday to Friday: 9:00 a.m. to 1:00 p.m. and 2:00 p.m. to 5:00 p.m. or 5:30 p.m.
- Some offices are open on Saturday: 9:00 a.m. to 1:00 p.m.

Government Offices

- Monday to Friday: 8:00 a.m. to 1:00 p.m. and 2:00 p.m. to 5:00 p.m.
- Saturday: 8:00 a.m. to 1:00 p.m.

Banks

- Monday to Friday: 10:00 a.m. to 3:00 p.m.
- Saturday: 9:30 a.m. to 11:30 a.m.

Stores

- Daily: 10:30 a.m. to 9:30 p.m. or 10:00 p.m.

HOLIDAYS & FESTIVALS

New Year's Day....................January 1
Chinese New Year....................January 26
Hari Raya Puasa....................March/April*
Good Friday....................March/April*
Labour Day....................May 1
Vesak Day....................May*
Hari Raya Haji....................June/July*
National Day....................August 9
Diwali....................October/November*
Christmas Day....................December 25

*date varies

THE PEOPLE

Ethnic Groups

- 76% Chinese (comprised of more than five subgroups with different dialects and different cultures).
- 15% Malay (indigenous to Singapore).
- 6% Indian (comprised of immigrants from India, Bangladesh, Pakistan, Sri Lanka and Myanmar).
- Less than 1% are European.
- Relations between all ethnic groups is good.

Language

- Singapore has four official languages: Malay, Tamil, Chinese, and English.
- Malay is the national language.
- Despite the fact that English is not the mother tongue for any of the three main ethnic groups, it is the primary language used in business, administration, commerce, and tourism.
- The Government of Singapore uses Mandarin Chinese.
- English is considered an important unifying factor because of its neutrality as well as its being the major international language.
- All Singaporeans are expected to learn English.
- The government strives to ensure that traditional cultures and values are maintained by encouraging use of all languages.
- The Chinese speak a number of different dialects. However, the government is encouraging all Chinese to learn and speak Mandarin.
- Most Singaporeans are bilingual or multilingual.

Religion

- Singapore has no official religion. Freedom of worship is constitutionally guaranteed.
- The major religions are Buddhism, Taoism, Confucianism, Islam, Christianity, Hinduism, and Judaism. A number of other smaller religions are also practiced.
- Approximately 50% (primarily Chinese) practice Buddhism or Taoism (or a combination of Buddhism, Taoism, and Confucianism).
- Most of the indigenous Malays are Muslim.
- The Chinese community believes in *Feug shui* (pronounced fung shway). The words mean "wind and water". *Feug shui* is an entire school of environmental and cultural doctrines. *Feug shui* is based on the premise that people experience happier, healthier, more prosperous lives when their homes and work environments are harmonious. New ventures or new construction will often require the blessing of a *Feug shui* master.

CONDUCTING BUSINESS

Meeting & Greeting

- Although Singapore has three major ethnic groups, each with its own tradition, the most common greeting is a handshake.
- The handshake is usually quite soft and lingering. Both hands may be used.
- Foreign businesswomen may shake hands with both men and women. Singaporean men will often wait for the woman to initiate the gesture.

Singaporean Chinese

- Singaporean Chinese may accompany their handshake with a nod of the head, particularly when greeting older people.

Singaporean Malay

- Singaporean Malay are often Muslim.
- Muslim tradition dictates that there is no public contact between the sexes.
- Devote Muslim men will ritually cleanse after they have touched a woman.
- If the Singaporean Malay is very westernized, he may shake hands with a woman.
- Foreign businesswoman should wait for a Malay man to initiate the gesture.
- Foreign businessmen should wait for a Singaporean Malay woman to offer her hand.
- The traditional Malay greeting is the *Salaam* that involves taking the right hand, touching the heart, then the forehead and then gesturing forward. It is not recommended that foreigners use this greeting.
- Some Muslims, particularly men, may bring their hands back to touch their chests after shaking hands to symbolize that the greeting comes from the heart. They are pleased when a foreigner reciprocates the gesture.

Singaporean Indian

- Although not common, Singaporean Indians may greet you in the traditional manner called a *namaste* (pronounced na-mas-tay), which is done by holding the palms of your hands together (as in a prayer) below the chin, accompanied by a slight nod.
- Many Singaporean Indians are Hindu.
- Traditionally, there is no public contact between the sexes.
- Only westernized Hindus will shake hands with women.
- A *namaste* in this situation is an acceptable alternative to a handshake for a foreign businesswoman.
- Business cards are exchanged at the beginning of a meeting.
- Cards should be given and received using both hands.
- It is not necessary to have your card translated into Mandarin on the back unless you are dealing with a Chinese company.
- You should begin meetings with a few minutes of casual conversation. Business discussions will usually begin relatively quickly.
- Avoid scheduling meetings during the luncheon period from 1:00 p.m. to 2:00 p.m.
- Avoid scheduling business trips during the Chinese New Year period.

Forms of Address

- The three different ethnic groups should each be addressed in a different manner.
- Because of the complexities, it is acceptable to ask a Singaporean how he or she wishes to be addressed.

Singaporean Chinese

- In Chinese names, the family name is traditionally placed first, followed by the given name.
- Address Chinese using their professional title (Engineer, Dr., President, etc.) or government title (Mayor, Councillor, etc.) followed by their family name.
- If the title is unknown, use the appropriate courtesy title (Mr., Mrs., or Miss) and their family name.
- Never address a Chinese by his or her family name alone.
- Traditionally, Chinese wives retain their maiden name. Marital status is indicated by using Madam or Mrs.
- Many Chinese have taken an English first name or use their initials to ease communications with English speakers.
- It is acceptable to ask how someone wishes to be addressed, if unsure about which is the family or first name.
- Only family members or close friends use first names.
- There are only 100 widely used family names. The five most common surnames are "Chang", "Wang", "Li", "Chao", and "Liu".

Singaporean Malays

- There are no family names. A man is known by his given name(s) followed by bin (son of) and his father's name.
- A woman is known by her given name(s) followed by *binte* (daughter of) and her father's name.
- To address a Malay, use the appropriate professional title (Dr., Professor, Engineer) or Mr./Mrs./Miss followed by their given name.
- The traditional greeting for Muslim men is *Encik* (pronounced onchik) followed by their first name. For a married woman it is *Puan* (pronounced poo-ahn) or for a single woman, *Cik* (pronounced chik), followed by her first name. The current trend is to use *Puan* for any adult female.
- Some married women will drop their father's name and take their husband's name.
- Some westernized Malays have removed *bin* or *binti* from their name.
- If a man has completed his pilgrimage to Mecca, he will be addressed as *Tuan Haji.*
- If a women has completed her pilgrimage to Mecca, she will be addressed as *Puan Hajah.*
- These honorific titles must be individually earned.

Singaporean Indians

- Professional titles (Doctor, Professor) or the English courtesy titles (Mr., Mrs. or Miss) plus the family name unless familiar with the Hindu, Muslim or Sikh greeting customs. Wait until invited to use first names.

Hindu:

- Given names come first, followed by family names.
- It is polite to use professional titles or *Shri* (Mr.); *Shrimati* Mrs.) or *Kumari* (Miss) or the suffix *–ji* with a last name to show respect.

Muslim:

- Muslims have no surname. A Muslim is generally known by a given name followed by *bin* (son of) or *binti* (daughter of) plus the father's given name.
- Married Muslim women do not always take the husband's name.

Sikhs:

- The given name is always followed by either *Singh* (for males) or *Kaur* (for females).
- All Sikhs use the name *Singh*, but not all Singhs are Sikhs.
- Address Sikhs by their professional title or Mr., Mrs., or Miss, and by their first name.
- To address a Sikh male as Mr. Singh is the equivalent of saying "Mr. Man" in English.

ENTERTAINING

- Business entertaining over lunch or dinner is common. Business breakfasts are rare.
- Most Singaporeans prefer to conduct business over lunches which can be long in duration.
- Business is often discussed over the meal.
- Do not invite a Singaporean business associate to lunch until you have had an opportunity to meet on a few occasions.
- Government officials may be prohibited from attending a social event.
- Spouses are often invited to dinners and other functions if business is not to be discussed.
- If you invite Singaporeans to dinner, ideally have an even number present at the table to ensure good fortune.
- You will rarely be invited to a Singaporean home for a business dinner.
- Shoes should be removed before entering most homes.

DINING ETIQUETTE

- Since Singapore has become quite westernized, the customs and eating etiquette will vary according to the cuisine and culture.
- Hindus and Buddhists do not eat beef; Muslims do not eat pork.
- Chopsticks are the most popular utensil although Western-style utensils are normally available.
- In most cases, diners will have individual bowls (plates or even a banana leaf) of rice.
- Wait until your host begins eating and invites you to start.
- Small amounts of food should be taken throughout the meal from communal platters.
- It is considered polite to always leave a little bit of food on the serving dishes (not in your own bowl or plate) to show that an adequate amount of food has been served and you have been well fed.

Singaporean Chinese

- At a round table, the guest of honour is always placed facing the entrance and to the host's left.
- Use chopsticks for eating and a porcelain spoon for soup.
- Chopsticks, when not in use, should be left on the chopstick rest. It is considered improper to rest them on your dinner plate or on the rice bowl. Do not place them standing straight up in the rice (associated with a funeral ritual and synonymous with death).
- Do not place bones, seeds or other debris in your rice bowl. If a separate dish is unavailable, they should be placed on the table.
- To remove any bones from your mouth, do not use your fingers. It is considered impolite. Most Chinese will use chopsticks to remove bones and then set them on a bone plate or on the table.

Singaporean Malay/Indian

- The guest of honour is usually seated at the head of the table or to the right of the host.
- Diners wash and dry their hands before and after a meal.
- When dining with Indians, always go to the washroom to wash your hands before eating.
- Malays will usually offer a small bowl and towel at the table.
- Malays and Indians eat using the fingers of their right hand.
- Never use your left hand as it is considered unclean.
- Forks and spoons may be used for some foods.
- If given a spoon and fork, hold the spoon in your right hand and the fork in your left; use the fork to push food onto the spoon.
- Always use a serving spoon, rather than your fingers, to take food from a communal dish.
- It is offensive to offer food (even to a family member) from your plate to others. Never let the serving spoon touch your plate. Indians believe that anything that touches someone's plate is polluted.
- Orthodox Muslims and most Hindus do not consume alcohol.
- It is customary for Malays to entertain at home rather than in restaurants.

PUNCTUALITY

- It is important to be punctual for business or social events.
- If you are going to be delayed for a meeting, you should phone ahead.

USEFUL PHRASES

- For Mandarin phrases, refer to the chapter on China.
- For Malay phrases, refer to the chapter on Malaysia.
- The Indian dialect spoken in Singapore is primarily Tamil rather than Hindi. For Tamil phrases, refer to the chapter on Sri Lanka.

VALUES AND SOCIAL CONVENTIONS

- Singapore has the highest standard of living in Southeast Asia.
- Singapore is one of the safest countries in Asia.
- British colonial influence is evident in many parts of Singapore society.
- Singaporeans are highly disciplined.
- Great value is placed on excellence, hard work, honesty, and education.
- The ethnic groups within Singapore peacefully coexist. Singapore is a country of racial harmony and national unity.
- Each ethnic group works hard to maintain its own cultural traditions.
- The family is central to all ethnic groups.
- Elders are respected.
- Singaporeans are usually modest and humble. Compliments are appreciated but are usually modestly denied.
- Loud voices and public displays of anger are frowned upon.
- The preservation of harmony is important.
- Singaporeans will not say an outright "no", as it is considered disrespectful. Common expressions used instead are "It is difficult" or "I would like to but..." or "maybe".
- The answer "yes" does not always indicate an affirmative. "Yes" may mean "Yes, I understand" or "Yes, I hear you".
- The concept of "saving face" is important in Chinese culture. "Face" refers to a person's pride, self-respect, family honour, and reputation. "Keeping face" means avoiding embarrassment, failure, or defeat.
- Be careful to avoid causing someone to "lose face" by insulting or criticizing him/her in public.
- Short periods of silence are common during discussions with Singaporeans. Be patient. Do not try to fill in the silence with further discussion. Await their response. Silence is not only considered polite, but may indicate serious thought.
- Do not be surprised by a laugh or smile at what may seem inappropriate times. This response may be used to mask feelings of embarrassment, nervousness, or other emotions.
- Very strict laws prohibit littering, jay walking, smoking, spitting, and chewing gum.
- Although most toilets now flush automatically, failure to flush a toilet is against the law.
- Punishment and fines can be severe, hence most Singaporeans respect and abide by the laws which have been established.

BODY LANGUAGE

- Public displays of affection are frowned upon.
- A woman may hold hands with another woman. This is considered a sign of friendship.
- Hitting your fist into your other cupped hand is considered obscene.
- Be sure to cover your mouth with your hand when yawning.
- It is considered rude to blow your nose or clear your throat in public.
- Minimize hand and body gestures when talking. Most Singaporeans find the movements distracting.
- Avoid touching someone's head (even to pat a child) as both Malays and Indians believe it is where the spirit or soul resides.
- For both Muslims and Hindus, the left hand is reserved for personal hygiene and therefore considered unclean. Do not eat, accept gifts, pass objects, or hold cash with your left hand. When both hands are needed, it is acceptable to use both.
- The foot is also considered unclean. Avoid showing the soles of your feet (or shoes), touching anyone or moving objects with your feet.
- When crossing your legs, do not place one ankle on the other knee.
- Shoes must always be removed before entering a mosque or temple.
- Do not point using your forefinger as Malaysians use this gesture to point only at animals. Even using two fingers is considered impolite by some Indians. Use the right hand, palm facing out or your right thumb (be sure the rest of your fingers are curled inward).
- It is a sign of anger if a person stands with hands on hips.
- An Indian may indicate agreement by a side-to-side toss of their head. Westerners often misinterpret this gesture to mean "no".
- A gesture which indicates someone is having difficulty giving a positive response, involves the sucking in of air or a hissing sound made through the teeth.
- To beckon someone, extend the arm out, hand down, and make a downward scratching motion with your fingers towards your body.
- It is considered polite to slightly bow when entering or leaving a room, or when passing by a group of people.

CONVERSATION

- Good topics include: Singapore's multicultural traditions, local cuisine and restaurants, favourite travel destinations, your trip to Singapore, positive remarks about the country, and your counterpart's overseas experiences.
- Topics to avoid include: discussions of a personal nature, local politics, racial friction, and religion. Avoid questioning your hosts about government policies.
- You may be asked what may appear to be "personal" questions such as your age, weight, and salary. This is not considered impolite to Singaporeans. If uncomfortable with any questions, remain polite but vague.

TIPPING

- Tipping is not expected and is often discouraged.
- In restaurants, a service charge is usually included in the bill.

DRESS & APPEARANCE

- Because Singapore is hot and humid all year around, you will need light-weight clothing.
- Sudden rain showers occur throughout the year. Bring an umbrella.
- Natural fabrics that breathe, such as cotton, are appropriate.
- Because of the heat, business dress in Singapore is somewhat casual.
- Foreign businessmen should dress more conservatively until aware of the formality required. Men should wear a suit and tie. Jackets may be removed if it seems appropriate.
- Foreign businesswomen should wear tailored linen and silk dresses or suits (pant suits are acceptable) with stockings and pumps. Avoid sleeveless garments. Short sleeves are acceptable.
- Singapore offices are often air-conditioned to extreme coldness so visitors should have a jacket handy.
- For business, Singaporean men will often wear dark trousers, a light-coloured long sleeved shirt and tie, without a jacket. Open-necked batik shirts are also popular.
- Singaporean businesswomen will wear either a light-coloured blouse with a skirt or a business suit, depending upon the formality of the office.

- The dress code at evening receptions can be business attire or "smart casual".
- Jeans are acceptable for both sexes.

GIFTS

- Business gifts are generally not exchanged.
- Gifts are exchanged between friends.
- A gift may be misinterpreted as a bribe, if it is given before a close relationship has been established.
- Singapore has very stringent laws against bribery.
- Government officials may not accept any gift.
- Each ethnic group has different gift-giving traditions.
- Gifts are never opened in the presence of the giver. To open a gift immediately indicates that the person is greedy. Gifts are put aside to be opened later.
- Gifts should be elegantly wrapped.
- When you wrap your gifts, be aware of the significance of colour for the different cultures in Singapore. See below.
- If invited to a private home for dinner, always bring a small gift.
- Give brand name, high quality gifts.

Singaporean Chinese

- Present your gift using both hands.
- In order not to appear greedy, Chinese will normally decline a gift several times before accepting. It is important to insist until they accept the gift.
- Similarly, you should decline several times before taking a gift.

Gift taboos include:

- clocks (associated with death),
- knives (negative connotations),
- green hats (a Chinese wearing a green hat indicates that his wife or girlfriend has been unfaithful),
- blankets (suppress prosperity), or
- handkerchiefs (symbolize grief and parting).

- Wrapping paper: Avoid white, black, and blue paper (associated with funerals). Red and gold are good colours to use as they are considered festive colours.

Singaporean Malay

- Do not give liquor, pork items, or knives.
- As Malays consider dogs unclean, do not give toy dogs or gifts that picture dogs.
- Wrapping paper: Avoid white paper (associated with funerals) or yellow paper (reserved for royalty).

Singaporean Indian

- Present gifts using the right hand.
- Wrapping paper: Green, red, and yellow are good colours to use.

FOR WOMEN

- Singapore is a very good place for foreign businesswomen to do business.
- Singaporean women are often highly educated and actively involved in business and commerce. However, there are still few females in top executive positions.
- Most Singaporean women managers are employed in personnel, administration, consumer affairs, and public relations. Most are in lower- and middle- management positions and support functions.

USEFUL ADDRESSES

World Trade Centre Singapore
1 Maritime Square, #09-72
WTC Building
Singapore 099253
Republic of Singapore

Fax: (65) 274-0721
Tel: (65) 274-7111
Email: wtcs@psa.com.sg
Website:
http://www.psa.com.sg/wtc

YOUR CULTURAL IQ

Q

In Western culture, it is common to use a crooked index finger to beckon someone. In most parts of the world, however, this gesture is considered inappropriate and in some countries offensive. What gesture is more commonly used?

A

In most countries around the world, the appropriate way to beckon someone is by extending the hand out, palm down, and making a scratching motion towards the body. In Malaysia, beckoning with the finger is only used for animals.

SRI LANKA

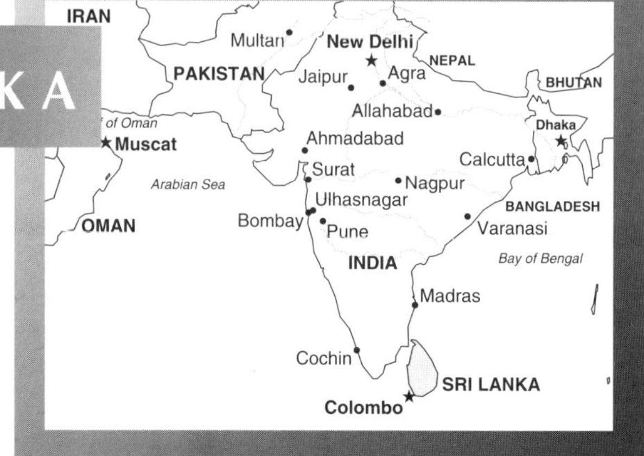

THE COUNTRY

Population
- 18.9 million

Capital
- Sri Jayawardhanapura
- Colombo is the commercial capital (1.3 million)

Government
- Unitary Multiparty Republic

Climate
- The climate is tropical.
- In inland areas, the humidity can rise as high as 85%
- Temperature average 27C (80F) year-round.
- Highland areas are cooler but also receive more rain than lowland regions.
- Snow has never been recorded on the mountain peaks of Sri Lanka.
- The two main seasons are summer and the monsoons.
- The summer season is from October to December. Temperatures may reach as high as 37C (99F).
- The two monsoon periods are: April to July and Mid-October to Mid-February (overlapping the summer months).

Electricity
- 230 to 240 volts
- Outlets require plugs with either two thin round pins or three round prongs.

Sports
- Sri Lankans enjoy a number of sports introduced by the British.
- Cricket is the most popular sport.
- Soccer, rugby, horse racing, table tennis, volleyball and netball (for girls) are also played.

Currency
- The Sri Lankan *rupee* (Rs.)

BUSINESS HOURS

Business & Government Offices
- Monday to Friday: 8:30 a.m. to 4:30 p.m.
- One hour is taken for lunch.
- Some businesses are open on Saturday morning.

Banks
- Monday: 9:00 a.m. to 1:00 p.m.
- Tuesday to Friday: 9:00 a.m. to 1:30 p.m.
- May close early just before public holidays.

Private Banks
- Monday to Friday: 9:00 a.m. to 3:00 p.m.

Stores
- Monday to Friday: 8:00 a.m. or 9:00 a.m. to 5:00 p.m.
- Many are open on Saturday mornings.

HOLIDAYS & FESTIVALS

- Sri Lanka celebrates many holidays. The most common holiday is "Poya Day", which occurs about every 28 days and marks the monthly full moon (a significant day for Buddhists).
- Each major religion has at least one national holiday.
- Check with the diplomatic or tourist offices to verify holiday dates before planning a visit.

Full Moon Poya Day..........January*
Tamil Thai-Pongal Day..........January 14
Id al-Fitr..........January*
Independence Commemoration Day..........February 4
Full Moon Poya Day..........February*
Maha Shivarathri Day..........February 25
Full Moon Poya Day..........March*
Id al-Adha..........April 8
Easter..........March/April*
Full Moon Poya Day..........April*

Sinhala and Tamil New Year's Eve.......April 13
Sinhala and Tamil New Year's..............April 14
May Day..May*
Full Moon Poya Day..................................May 11
Day After Vesak Full Moon
Poya Day...May*
Full Moon Poya Day..................................June*
Special Bank Holiday..............................June 30
Holy Prophet's Birthday............................July 7
Full Moon Poya Day....................................July*
Full Moon Poya Day...............................August*
Full Moon Poya Day........................September*
Full Moon Poya Day..............................October*
Deepavali Festival Day.......................October 19
Full Moon Poya Day..........................November*
Full Moon Poya Day..........................December*
Christmas.......................................December 25
Special Bank Holiday....................December 31

*date varies

THE PEOPLE

Ethnic Groups

- 74% are Sinhalese (concentrated in the southwest)
- Tamils (generally concentrated in the north, the "tea" region):
- 12% Ceylon Tamils
- 6% Indian Tamils
- 7% Moors (locally called Muslims)
- 1% Malays, Burghers (descendants of Dutch colonists), and Veddahs (remnants of islands original inhabitants).
- Severe ethnic tensions exist between the Sinhalese and Tamils. There have been outbursts of violence since the early 1980's.

Language

- The official languages of Sri Lanka are Sinhala and Tamil.
- English (a legacy from the colonial period) is the primary language of commerce and is spoken by approximately 10% of the population.
- Most business people and civil servants speak English fluently.
- English is spoken in the tourist areas.

Religion

- 69.3% of the population practice Theravada Buddhism.
- 15.5% are Hindu.
- 7.6% are Christian.
- 7.5% are Muslim.
- 93% of the Sinhalese are Buddhist.
- More than 80% of Ceylon and Indian Tamils are Hindu.
- All Moors are Muslim.
- Burghers, Eurasians, and some Sinhalese and Tamils are Christian.
- Freedom of worship has been guaranteed by the Constitution.
- Special status has been given by the government to Buddhism.

CONDUCTING BUSINESS

Meeting & Greeting

- Greetings can vary between the ethnic groups.
- The most common greeting is similar to the Indian namaste. Both hands are placed together, as in prayer, slightly below the chin. This is accompanied by a slight bowing of the head.
- Most Sri Lankan business people will greet foreign visitors with a handshake.
- One should wait for a Sri Lankan women to offer her hand.
- Common verbal greetings are the Sinhalese phrase *Ayubowan or* or the Tamil *Vannakkam.*
- Both expressions mean "May you be blessed with the gift of a long life".
- When responding with a bow, an appropriate verbal response is the Sinhalese phrase *Aaibowan* or the Tamil *Namaste.*
- Both expressions mean "I salute the god-like qualities within you".
- Business cards are always exchanged.
- If you can distinguish between Sinhalese and Tamil, it is a good idea to have the cards printed with the local language on the reverse side.
- Begin meetings with casual conversation. The Sri Lankans enjoy talking.
- Do not schedule meetings toward the end of the day, as business people often leave their offices before the official day ends at 4:30 p.m.
- Appointments should be made at least two weeks in advance. Reconfirm the meeting a day or two before the appointed date.

Forms of Address

- Whether you are addressing a Sinhalese, Burgher, Tamil, or Muslim, the family is the last name.
- Addressing someone using the English courtesy titles (Mr., Mrs., or Miss) plus the last name is acceptable.

- Sri Lankans are highly conscious of titles. When possible, use them when addressing acquaintances.
- Use the title Doctor for medical doctors or those who hold degrees.
- A Sinhalese person may be addressed as *Mahattaya* (sir) or *Nona* (madam) following his/her last name or simply with this title alone.
- For Tamils, it is customary to use *Aiyaa* (father) or *Amaa* (mother) when addressing an older person to show respect.
- Each ethnic group prefers to be addressed differently. Be sure to ask what he/she would like to be addressed as.

ENTERTAINING

- Meal times are 7:00 a.m. to 8:00 a.m. for breakfast,12:00 noon and 2:00 p.m. for lunch, and between 7:00 p.m. and 10:00 p.m. for dinner.
- Initial meetings are often held over a meal (particularly lunch).
- The person who extends the invitation, pays for the meal.
- It is common for Sri Lankans to invite a foreign visitor to their home for a visit or a meal.
- Shoes are often removed before entering a home.
- Generally, there is social conversation for two or three hours before the meal is served. People tend to leave within a half-hour of completion of the meal.
- When invited to a home, guests are often served tea (usually sweetened with milk and sugar). It is impolite to refuse, but acceptable to ask for a different kind of beverage.
- Most Sri Lankans drink water and wash their hands in a bowl of water following a meal.
- Be sensitive to food restrictions. Buddhists do not eat flesh (although some will eat fish or eggs). Hindus do not eat beef or pork. Muslims do not eat pork.

DINING ETIQUETTE

- Traditionally food is eaten using the right hand. However, utensils are becoming common in hotels and restaurants.
- Bread and rice balls are used to scoop up curries and vegetables.
- A plantain leaf may be used as a plate (not to be eaten).
- Communal dishes are often placed in the center of the table. Guests serve themselves.
- Do not let serving utensils touch your plate.
- It is considered complimentary to your host if you eat a few servings of food. You should therefore take only small portions to give the opportunity to ask for second and third helpings.
- Additional servings, once you are finished, can be politely refused.

USEFUL PHRASES

Sinhala

Hello
(Halo)

Good morning
(Ayubowan)

Good afternoon
(Ayubowan)

Good evening
Ayubowan)

How are you?
(Kohomada)

Please
(Karunakara)

Thank you
(Istutiyi)

You are welcome
(Sadarayen Piliganima)

Yes
(Ou)

No
(Naa)

No, I do not understand
(Mata therenne nehe)

Good-bye
(English influence)

Cheers
(English influence)

Tamil

Hello
(Halo)

Good morning
(Vanakkam)

Good afternoon
(Vanakkam)

Good evening
(Vanakkam)

How are you?
(Eppadi irukkintrirgal)

Please
(Thayavu panni)

Thank you
(Nandri)

You are welcome
(Waravetkirem)

Yes
(Ome)

No
(Illai)

No, I do not understand
(Enakku vilanga illai)

Good-bye
(Vanakkam, pooi varagirein)

Cheers
(English influence)

VALUES AND SOCIAL CONVENTIONS

- Sri Lanka is correctly pronounced "SHREE-lanka".
- The name of the country was changed in 1972 from Ceylon to Sri Lanka (meaning "resplendent island").
- Although the caste system has been officially abolished, it is an integral part of Sri Lankan society.
- An individual's status within an ethnic group is dependent upon various factors, including skin colour, physical stature, economic standing and life-style.
- It is important to respect this aspect of the culture.
- In business, "tea breaks" are taken in the morning and the afternoon. No business is conducted during these periods.
- Business proceeds at a more leisurely pace than it does in North America.
- Interpersonal relationships are important for conducting business. Take the time to establish rapport with your Sri Lanka counterparts.
- When making business decisions, the Sinhalese are concerned with responsibility to self and to interpersonal relationships. The Tamils are concerned with the individual's responsibility to the group – the family, social group and religion. Thus, an individual's decision is made with social position in mind. An individual's rank within the group is also important.
- The family is central to life for both the Sinhalese and Tamils.
- Men and women still occupy very traditional roles. In most cases, men dominate all aspects of business and social life.
- Sri Lankan businessmen may consult an astrologist before making a business commitment.

BODY LANGUAGE

- The left hand is reserved for bodily hygiene and is therefore considered "unclean". Eat and touch other people using the right hand only. Pass objects to others using the right hand or both hands.
- Remove shoes and hat when entering a Buddhist temple or Hindu shrine.
- Any image of Buddha is considered sacred. Do not touch, lean or sit on one.
- Monks are not permitted to touch money. Cash donations should be placed in the box found at the temple's entrance.
- Women are forbidden to touch Buddhist monks.
- Both hands should be used when giving anything to a Buddhist monk.
- Both men and women should have their legs and arms covered when entering a mosque.
- Nodding the head up and down signifies "no", while shaking it back and forth indicates "yes". This is the reverse from the Western custom.
- Smiling is considered flirtatious. Sri Lankans tend to smile only when they are happy or wish to indicate thanks (in lieu of giving a verbal "thank you").
- Because the head is considered sacred (houses the soul), it is important not to touch anyone on the head (even to pat the head of a child).
- The feet are considered dirty. Do not point the sole of your foot at anyone. Do not use feet to move objects. Do not put feet on chairs or tables.

- Using the index finger to point or beckon someone is considered rude. To beckon a person, extend the hand out, palm down and make a scratching motion towards your body.
- It is considered impolite to pass between two people in conversation. If unavoidable, the passer should crouch slightly and give apologies.
- It is common to see people of the same sex holding hands in public.
- Members of the opposite sex, however, do not hold hands in public.

CONVERSATION

- Sports are an excellent topic of conversation.
- Other good topics include the sights of Sri Lanka, culture, your travels and your own country.
- Topics to avoid: relations with India, religion, the ethnic struggle between the Tamils and Sinhalese, the caste system, and the topic of sex.

TIPPING

- Tipping is common.
- The better restaurants automatically add a 10% service charge.
- Taxi drivers do not expect a tip.

DRESS & APPEARANCE

- Because of the warm climate, conservative lightweight clothing is appropriate.
- Businessmen should wear light shirts and trousers. Jackets and ties are rarely worn.
- A modest light blouse and skirt or dress is appropriate for businesswomen.
- Women should avoid wearing short, sleeveless or revealing clothing. This attire is only suitable for the beach or the resorts.
- Sri Lankans who live in the cities will often wear Western style attire. However, traditional forms of dress are still popular.
- Sri Lankan women may wear a *saree* with a light blouse, or a *redda* (a wraparound skirt) with a *hatte* (blouse).
- Traditional attire for Sri Lankan men is a *sarong* (piece of cloth wrapped around the waist) with a *banion* (sleevless shirt) or loose-fitting trousers with a shirt that has long, loose sleeves.

GIFTS

- Gift giving in the normal business context is not common or expected.
- Upon the completion of a deal, however, a tasteful gift is acceptable.
- If visiting a home, you are not expected to give a gift, but it is appreciated. Good gifts include: chocolates, fruit, and handicrafts from your home country.
- Both hands should be used when giving a gift to show respect.
- If only one hand is used for giving something, the belief is that it has not been given freely.

FOR WOMEN

- Although there are numerous women in business and government, few are found in top-level positions.
- Foreign businesswomen will be treated with courtesy and respect.

USEFUL ADDRESSES

World Trade Centre Colombo
Hospitality International (PVT) Ltd.
Level 18, East Tower
World Trade Center
Colombo 1, Sri Lanka

Fax: (94 1) 346 779
Tel: (94 1) 346 778/346 165
Email: wtlo@lankacom.net

YOUR CULTURAL IQ

Q **In what country would the gift of a green baseball hat be considered inappropriate?**

A In China, wearing a green hat indicates that your wife or girlfriend has been unfaithful.

Q **You and your Japanese friend are shopping and both of you admire some beautiful candlestick holders in a shop window. As a gift, you decide to give your friend a set of four of them. You find out later she was not happy with the gift. What happened?**

A There are lucky and unlucky numbers in every society. The Japanese and Chinese will go to great lengths to avoid using or giving items that are four in number. In both of these societies, the number "four" sounds like the word for "death".

TAIWAN

THE COUNTRY

Population
- 21.9 million
- 55% of the population are under the age of 30.

Capital
- Taipei (2.6 million)

Major Cities
- Kaohsing (1.4 million)
- Taichung (882,000)

Government
- Multi-party republic.
- President is the chief of state.
- Premier is the head of government.

Climate
- Taipei has a sub-tropical climate in the north and a tropical climate in the south.
- Taipei has unpleasantly cool, damp winters. Temperatures range from 12C (54F) to 21C (69F).
- Summer is long and humid. Temperatures range from 23C (74F) to 34C (92F).
- From November to March or mid-April, monsoon winds bring in heavy rains and a substantial decrease in temperature. Temperatures range from 14C (58F) to 29C (84F).
- From April to June, it is warm and mild but with frequent rains (plum rain). Worst months are May and June for rain.
- July to September is very hot and humid. This is the most likely period for typhoons.
- October and November are the most pleasant months. Temperatures range from 23C (74F) to 31C (89F).

Electricity
- 110 volts
- Electrical outlets require plugs with two flat parallel blades.

Sports
- Basketball, ping pong, volleyball, baseball, badminton, tennis and soccer are popular.
- Taiwan's Little League champions consistently do well in the Little League World Series.
- Taiwan has a professional baseball league.

Currency
- The *New Taiwan dollar* (NT$)

BUSINESS HOURS

Business Offices
- Monday to Friday: 8:30 a.m. or 9:00 a.m. to 5:00 p.m. or 5:30 p.m. (Many businesspeople work longer hours).
- Lunch break for 1 to 1 1/2 hours.
- Saturday: 8:30 a.m. to 12:30 p.m.

Government Offices
- Weekdays: 8:30 a.m. to 12:00 noon and 1:30 p.m. to 5:30 p.m.
- Saturday: 8:30 a.m. to 12:00 noon

Banks
- Weekdays: 9:00 a.m. to 3:30 p.m.
- Saturday: 9:00 a.m. to noon.

Stores
- Daily: 9:00 a.m. or 10:00 a.m. to 10:00 p.m.

HOLIDAYS & FESTIVALS

National Founding Day of the Republic of China.........January 1
Chinese Lunar New Year.........January/February*
Lantern Festival.........February 6
Youth Day.........March 29
Tomb Sweeping Day and Chiang Kai-shek's Memorial Day.........April 5
Dragon Boat Festival.........June*
Mid-Autumn (Moon Festival).........September*
Confucius' Birthday.........September 28
Double Tenth National Day.........October 10
Taiwan Restoration Day.........October 25
Birthday of President Chiang Kai-shek.........October 31
Birthday of Dr. Sun Yat-sen.........November 12*
Constitution Day.........December 25

*date varies

THE PEOPLE

Ethnic Groups

- 84% Taiwanese (descendants of migrants who left China between the 17th and 19th centuries).
- 14% Mainland Chinese (the Nationalist Chinese who came to Taiwan in 1949)
- 2% Aboriginal inhabitants of Taiwan. This group is comprised of several ethnic groups (which in many cases have retained their language and traditions).

Language

- The official language is Mandarin Chinese.
- Taiwanese (a southern Fukien dialect) is widely spoken.
- The written form of Chinese uses a simplified character system rather than the modernized Chinese script used in the People's Republic of China.
- English is a popular second or third language to study in school.
- English is widely used and understood by businesspeople.

Religion

- 93% of the population practice a combination of Buddhism, Confucianism, and Taoism.
- 4.5% of the population are Christians.
- 2.5% practice other religions.

CONDUCTING BUSINESS

Meeting & Greeting

- A smile and a nod of the head are customary when meeting someone for the first time.
- Handshakes are used between acquaintances and close friends.
- Adding a small bow is a sign of respect. Hands should be at your sides and your feet together.
- Among the foreign educated younger Taiwanese, a handshake is common. The handshake is generally soft and lingering. Occasionally, both hands may be used.
- Foreign businessmen should wait for a Taiwanese woman to offer her hand.
- Foreign businesswomen should initiate a handshake.
- A common Chinese verbal greeting is *Ni hao ma*, which means "How are you?" The polite response is *Nen hao, hsieh hsieh ni* (hen how, syeh syeh nee) which means "very well, thank you".
- Older people should be greeted first.
- You should always stand when an elderly person, or someone of high rank, enters or departs the room.
- Use the right hand or both hands to give business cards.
- The print on the card should face the recipient.
- Upon receiving a business card, be sure to take a moment to review the card (even if it is in Chinese only).
- If you are seated at a table, it is polite to place the card or cards on the table in front of you in order to refer to them.
- Do not write on a person's card while in their presence.
- Cards should be stored in a proper business card holder. Do not store a person's card in your wallet and then put it in your back pocket.
- Cards should be translated into Mandarin Chinese (preferably in gold ink – the most prestigious colour) on the reverse side. Be sure to have the translation done by a Taiwanese expert. The simplified script used in the People's Republic of China is not acceptable.
- Be sure to have on hand an ample supply of business cards. Cards are important as they indicate rank and ultimately the kind of respect you will receive. You will almost certainly "lose face" if you run out of cards.
- The most common Chinese greetings used for foreign visitors is "*Ni hao*" (Hello) or "*Ni hao ma?*" (How do you do?).
- Always begin meetings with pleasant casual conversation.

- Beverages (tea and coffee) will often be served. You should accept the offer and wait until you have finished your beverage before discussing business.
- Always allow your host to enter a room, elevator, or vehicle first.
- The best time to plan a business trip to Taiwan is between the months of April and September.
- Avoid trips to Taiwan during the period from January to March when most businesspeople take their vacations.
- Try to schedule appointments in the morning or after 2:00 p.m.
- Many Taiwanese take short naps after lunch (between 1:30 and 2:00 p.m.)
- A common rhetorical greeting is *"Have you eaten?"*. The polite response is "Yes" regardless of whether you have eaten. The question is rhetorical and not intended to elicit information.

Forms of Address

- In Chinese names, the family name is traditionally placed first, followed by the given name.
- Address Taiwanese using their professional title (Engineer, Dr., President, etc.) or government title (Mayor, Councillor, etc.) followed by their family name.
- If the title is unknown, use the appropriate courtesy title (Mr., Mrs., or Miss) and their family name.
- Never address a Taiwanese by his or her family name alone.
- Traditionally, Taiwanese wives retain their maiden name. Marital status is indicated by using Madam or Mrs.
- Many Taiwanese have taken an English first name or use their initials to ease communications with English speakers.
- It is acceptable to ask how someone wishes to be addressed if unsure about which is the family or first name.
- Only family members or close friends use first names.
- There are only 100 widely used family names. The five most common surnames are "Chang", "Wang", "Li", "Chao", and "Liu".

ENTERTAINING

- Entertaining is a critical part of Taiwan's business culture.
- Dinner and evening entertainment (visiting local night clubs or karaoke bars) should be expected.
- Business lunches are not common and business breakfasts are rare.
- The Taiwanese/Chinese are generous hosts. Banquets consisting of 12 to 20 courses are common.
- Banquets typically begin at 6:00 p.m. or 7:00 p.m. and last for two or more hours.
- Guests should arrive on time for banquets. Spouses are not usually included in business entertaining.
- Wait to be seated. Seating arrangements will be done according to rank.
- If seated at a round table, the guest of honour will be seated facing the door.
- Business is commonly discussed at social functions, but you should wait for your counterparts to initiate the conversation.
- Conversations during dinner usually focus on the meal itself (how it was prepared and the ingredients).
- Show appreciation for the food served. The Taiwanese are proud of their cuisine.
- Do not offer to share the restaurant bill with the Taiwanese.
- The Taiwanese will rarely entertain at home. It is an honour to be a guest.
- If invited to a private home, you should remove your shoes before entering the house.
- Foreign business visitors are not expected to reciprocate a banquet. However, should you decide to do so, an invitation to a very good Chinese restaurant or Western-style restaurant just prior to the end of a business trip is appropriate.

DINING ETIQUETTE

- Use chopsticks for eating and a porcelain spoon for soup.
- Attempt to use chopsticks. The Taiwanese will appreciate it.
- Chopsticks, when not in use, should be left on the chopsticks rest or on the table. Do not place them parallel on the top of your bowl (considered bad luck) or standing straight up in the rice (associated with a funeral ritual and synonymous with death).
- Dropping your chopsticks is considered bad luck.

- It is considered rude to tap your chopsticks on the table.
- When eating rice, bring the bowl close to your mouth.
- Do not refuse any food, as this may be considered impolite. If you don't want to eat something, simply push it to the side of your dish.
- Sauces are for dipping. Do not pour them into your rice bowl.
- If dining in a restaurant, you will be served dinner at a round table with dishes in the center on a revolving tray.
- Wait for the host to start eating before you begin.
- Do not place bones, seeds or other debris in your rice bowl. If a separate dish is unavailable, they should be placed on the table.
- Leave a small amount of rice in your bowl when you have finished the meal. An empty bowl will indicate a need for more rice.
- Toasting is customary. The host will make toasts before and during the meal.
- Your host may drink a toast to you and then pass you the empty glass. The glass will be refilled by one of the hosts. Using this glass, you should toast your hosts and then drink the whisky or wine.
- Tea is served at the end of the meal.
- Leave promptly after the meal is finished.

PUNCTUALITY

- It is important to be punctual for all meetings. Call if you are delayed. Do not get upset if your counterpart is late.
- Allow extra transit time when scheduling meetings in Taipei due to the heavy traffic.

USEFUL PHRASES

Yes
Dui
(Doo-ee)

No
Bu shi
(Boo shi)

Please
Qing
(Chying)

Thank you
Xie xie
(Syeh syeh)

You are welcome
Bu xie
(Boo syeh)

Hello
Ni hao
(Nee how)

Hello (phone)
Wei
(Way)

Good morning (until 10:00 a.m.)
Zao
(Dzow)

Good afternoon/evening
Ni Hao or Wanan
(Nee how or Wahn-ahn)

Good night
Wanan
(Wahn-ahn)

Good bye
Zaijan
(Dzigh-jyen)

Excuse me (when asking a question)
Qing wen
(Chying wen)

Excuse me (to get by someone)
Lao jia
(Laow jyee-ah)

Excuse me (I'm sorry)
Duibuqi
(Doo-ee-boo-chyee)

VALUES AND SOCIAL CONVENTIONS

- Taiwan formed its own government in 1949 after the Chinese Nationalist Party under Chiang Kai-shek lost a civil war in China to the Communist party. Chiang fled to Formosa (name given in the 1600's by the Portuguese, which meant "Beautiful Island) which was renamed Taiwan.
- Taiwan's present name means "Terraced Bay" in Chinese.
- References to the PRC and "Greater China" should be avoided. One should never refer to Taiwan as the People's Republic of China. Taiwan's official name is the Republic of China (ROC).
- Establish contacts before you go. In Taiwan, it is important to have connections or *guanxi* (pronounced gwahn-shee). The Taiwanese spend a considerable

amount of time and effort establishing and nurturing their connections. To succeed in Taiwan, it is important for foreign businesspeople to build up their own *guanxi.*

- Confucianism has had a great influence on Taiwan society.
- The family, including extended family and friends, is central to Taiwanese life.
- Family needs take precedence over the individual. Family loyalty is of the utmost importance.
- Always treat the elderly with respect. Do not wear sunglasses, or smoke in their presence. They should be acknowledged first in group settings. It is considered polite to allow them to go ahead of you when passing through a doorway.
- The concept of "saving face" is very important in Taiwanese culture. "Face" refers to a person's pride, self-respect, family honour, and reputation. "Keeping face," means avoiding embarrassment, failure, or defeat.
- Be careful to avoid causing someone to "lose face" by insulting or criticizing him/her in public.
- The Taiwanese find it difficult to say "no". To save face or maintain harmony, the Taiwanese/Chinese will respond with "we shall see", "maybe" or with some other indirect reply.
- Harmony must be maintained. Expect the Taiwanese to always say yes, although it may sometimes indicate no. "Yes" may sometimes be interpreted as "yes, I understand" or "yes, I hear you".
- Getting straight to the point and being blunt is not appreciated in Taiwan. A direct "no" is considered rude.
- Foreign visitors should be conscious about "numbers" when conducting business in Taiwan.
- The Taiwanese, like many Asians, are superstitious about numbers. The number 4 is considered unlucky in Taiwan because the word for "four" sounds like the word for "death".
- The number 5 is considered unlucky for the Taiwanese, as it sounds like the word for "mistake".
- The numbers 3,6, and 8 are considered favourable numbers. Three represents life and 8 indicates prosperity.
- Setting a date for the signing of a contract or a celebration dinner should be discussed with your Taiwanese counterparts to ensure that the dates are considered fortuitous.
- The Taiwanese consider strong public displays of emotions (anger, annoyance, or embarrassment) as a loss of self-control. Public displays of anger will result in "loss-of-face".
- Business in Taiwan is fast paced.
- Hard work is considered a virtue, particularly for the older generation. Ten-hour (or more) workdays are common.
- The Taiwanese do not like dust. It is common to see motorcyclists and bicyclists wearing surgical masks to protect themselves from dust.
- Modesty is important. It is considered impolite to boast. Downplay your achievements and possessions. Allow your promotional materials to give information about you and your company's success. Compliments should be politely refuted.
- Most Taiwanese/Chinese are modest and humble. They are unlikely to respond to a compliment. This should not prevent you from complimenting them, as compliments are always appreciated.
- In all forms of business, humility is crucial.
- Avoid overly admiring an object as it may result in the individual feeling obligated to give it to you.
- Central to many Chinese religious beliefs is *Feng shui* (pronounced fung shway), The words mean "wind and water". *Feng shui* has been practiced for over three thousand years in China. *Feng shui* is an entire school of environmental and cultural doctrines. *Feng shui* is based on the premise that people experience happier, healthier, more prosperous lives when their homes and work environments are harmonious. New ventures or new construction will often require the blessing of a *Feng shui* master.

BODY LANGUAGE

- Always hand a piece of paper to someone using both hands. It shows respect. Using only one hand is considered rude.
- Because conformity is valued over individualism, being "left-handed" is considered odd.
- The left hand is not considered unclean (as is the custom in Muslim countries).
- Shoes should be removed before entering a home.
- In private homes, special slippers or shoes are often provided for using the toilet facilities.
- The gesture to indicate the number "10", is two index fingers crossed. If you hold up ten fingers to indicate the number 10, you will not be understood.
- It is consider improper for adults to eat or drink while walking on the street.
- A gesture used to indicate "no", is made with the hand perpendicular in front of the face (not touching it), palm out, and waving it back and forth.
- Refrain from touching the Taiwanese. The Taiwanese tend to shun bodily contact with strangers.
- Do not touch someone's head (even to pat a child) as the head is considered the spiritual part of the person.
- Taiwanese will point to their nose to refer to themselves when speaking.
- To beckon someone, extend your hand with the palm down and move fingers in a scratching motion towards the body. Never use the index finger to beckon anyone.
- Winking is considered rude.
- It is common to see young women walking hand-in-hand in public. It is regarded as a sign of friendship.
- Hands should be placed in your lap when sitting.
- Traditionally, public displays of affection between men and women was frowned upon, but this is beginning to change.
- Placing your fingers in your mouth, for whatever reason, is seen as an unclean gesture that should be avoided.
- Maintaining good posture is important.
- Feet should not be used to point at something or to move objects.
- Never put your feet on a desk or chair.
- Men should not cross their legs. Both feet should be kept on the floor.
- Do not point using the index finger, as it considered rude. The Taiwanese point with an open hand.
- The Taiwanese, if they are nervous or embarrassed, may attempt to disguise their emotions by smiling or laughing.
- The Taiwanese may cover their faces with their hands when they are embarrassed.

CONVERSATION

- Good topics include your travels, the weather, an appreciation for the significant economic gains that Taiwan has achieved, or your country. It is considered polite to inquire about someone's health.
- Topics to avoid: politics, communism, discussions regarding mainland China or a reunification with mainland China. Avoid referring to Taiwan as an independent country or nation, as technically at least, it remains a province of China. Ask questions rather than making unsolicited comments. China should be referred to as the "mainland" during any discussions to avoid offense.
- Personal questions may sometimes be asked (for example, are you married, how many children do you have, and how much money do you make?). Asking personal questions is considered friendly. If you find the question uncomfortable, it is acceptable to politely respond that it is not your custom to discuss such things.

TIPPING

- Hotels: A 10% service charge is usually included.
- Restaurants: A 10% service charge is usually included. A modest tip is usually left at major, expensive Chinese and Western restaurants.
- Room service and other staff: 10% is appropriate.
- Taxis: Small change for good service or handling luggage.

- Toilet attendants: NT$5 to NT$10
- Coat check attendants: NT$10 to NT$50
- Porters: NT$50 to NT$100 per bag
- Hairdressers, barbers, drivers: NT$50 to NT$100

DRESS & APPEARANCE

Business

- Men should wear a conservative suit and tie.
- Women should wear a conservative suit in any colour (although dark colours, such as grey or navy blue, are appropriate for "power suits"). Low heel shoes and minimal amounts of jewellery are recommended.
- Purses and briefcases are considered status symbols, so should therefore be of a good brand.
- Women should avoid wearing black or white clothing, as these colours are associated with funeral attire.

Casual

- Attire should be modest. Women should not wear revealing clothing.

Social events

- Women should not wear black to a wedding (associated with funerals).
- Pack an umbrella or raincoat if visiting during the summer months. Rain showers are frequent.
- Businesspeople in Taipei are very fashion oriented.
- Most international businesspeople will be dressed in quality, top-of-the-line business attire.

GIFTS

- Gift giving is common in business.
- Seek advice before initiating gift giving. While appropriate on certain occasions, it is sometimes unnecessary and the recipient may feel obliged to reciprocate.
- Gifts should be given and received using both hands.
- The gift is not opened in the presence of the giver.
- Gifts should always be wrapped.
- Avoid the colours white, blue or black for wrapping paper (associated with death).
- Because the colour red is very auspicious. Red and gold are good colours to use for wrapping paper. Do not wrap gifts prior to your arrival in Taiwan, as they may be opened by customs.
- Moderately priced business gifts include: gold pens, illustrated books from your region, imported liquor, magazine subscriptions, chocolates, and company logo gifts.
- Be sure the products were not manufactured in Taiwan.
- If invited to a home for a meal, avoid bringing "food" gifts. Giving food may imply that your host cannot provide enough. Food can be sent after the event, along with a thank you note. Chocolate, candy, or fruit baskets are appropriate.

Gift taboos include:

  - clocks (associated with death),
  - knives (negative connotations),
  - green hats (a Chinese wearing a green hat indicates that his wife or girlfriend has been unfaithful),
  - blankets (suppress prosperity), or
  - handkerchiefs (symbolize grief and parting).

- If giving flowers, be sure not to give an "odd" number which is considered unlucky.
- Be conscious of the importance of "numbers" when giving gifts. Do not give gifts that are four in number or that add up to four (such as two pairs of socks).
- Gifts are often given in pairs.
- Gifts in sets of 2, 6, or eight are good. Eight is considered particularly auspicious.
- In Chinese culture, it is traditional for the recipient to refuse the gift two or three times before accepting (to avoid being seen as greedy). Insist until the gift is accepted. It is not necessary for a foreigner to adopt this practice when offered a gift.
- Gifts are never opened in the presence of the giver. They are politely put aside to be opened later.
- Do not wrap your gifts until after you have arrived. Customs officials may open packages.

FOR WOMEN

- Although Taiwan is a male dominated society, foreign businesswomen will have no difficulty conducting business here.
- Foreign businesswomen will be invited to dinners, but often not to the evening entertainment.
- Women in Taiwan are active in business and the professions.
- However, there are few women in politics and in high-level positions in business.

USEFUL ADDRESSES

Taipei World Trade Center Co., Ltd.
3rd-8th Floor, CETRA Tower
333 Keelung Road, Section 1
Taipei 110, Taiwan

Fax: (886 2) 2757-6653
Tel: (886 2) 2725-5200
Email: centra@centra.org.tw
Website: http://www.twtc.org.tw

World Trade Center Taichung
60 Tienpao Street
Taichung 407, Taiwan

Fax: (886 4) 358-2341
Tel: (886 4) 358-2271
Email: wtctxg@ms1.hinet.net

THAILAND

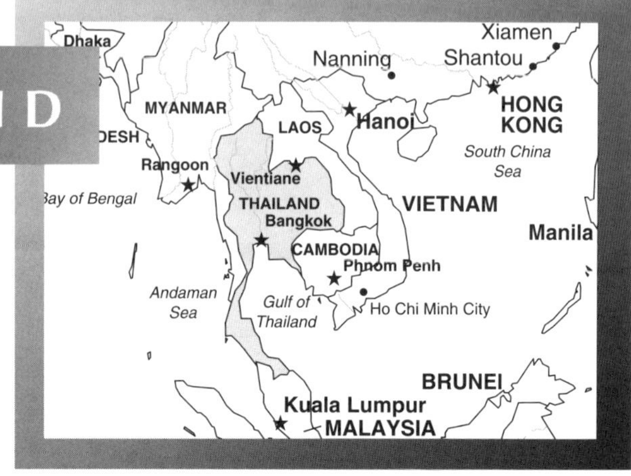

THE COUNTRY

Population
- 60 million

Capital
- Bangkok (6.5 million)

Government
- Constitutional monarchy
- The king is the head of state.
- The prime minister is the head of government.

Climate
- Thailand experiences three seasons.
- The hot and humid summer season is March to May. Temperatures range from 24C (75F) to 35C (95F).
- The cooler dry season is November to February. Temperatures range from 20C (68F) to 33C (91F).
- The hot, rainy monsoon period is from June to October. Temperatures range from 24C (75F) to 35C (95F).

Electricity
- 220 volts
- Electrical outlets require plugs with either two flat parallel blades or two thin round pins.

Sports
- Popular sports are soccer, table tennis, badminton, and volleyball.

Currency
- The *baht* (B)

BUSINESS HOURS

Business Offices
- Monday to Friday: 8:30 a.m. to 5:00 p.m.

Government Offices
- Monday to Friday: 8:30 a.m. to 4:30 p.m.

Banks
- Monday to Friday: 8:30 a.m. to 3:30 p.m.

Stores
- Daily: 9:00 a.m. or 10:00 a.m. to 8:00 p.m.

Department stores
- Daily: 9:00 a.m. to 6:00 p.m. (sometimes until 9:00 p.m.)

HOLIDAYS & FESTIVALS

New Year's Day	January 1
Chinese New Year	January/February*
Makhabucha Day	March 7
Chakri Day	April 6
Songhkran Day (Thai New Year)	April 13-15
Ploughing Ceremony	May 14
Labour Day	May 1
Coronation Day	May 5
Visakhabucha Day	May 29
Asalahabucha Day	July 27
Rains Retreat	July 28
Queen Sirikit's Birthday	August 12
Ok Pansa	October*
Chulalongkorn Day	October 23
King Bhumiphol's Birthday	December 5
Constitution Day	December 10
New Year's Eve	December 31

*date varies

THE PEOPLE

Ethnic Groups
- 75% of the population are connected with agriculture in some form.
- 10% of the total population reside in the city of Bangkok.
- 78% of the population are ethnic Thais.

- The ethnic Thai are comprised of Central Thai, North Eastern Thai, Northern Thai, and Southern Thai.
- Chinese, Mon, Khmer, Burmese, Malay, Lao, Persian and Indian strains are, to varying degrees, mixed with Thai stock.
- 13% of the population are Chinese.
- It is difficult to distinguish between the Chinese and Thai, as over several generations considerable intermarriage has occurred between the two groups.
- 9% of the population are comprised of ethnic minorities – primarily, northern hilltribes, Lao, Vietnamese and Cambodian refugees, as well as a number of South Asian Indian and other permanent foreign residents.

Language

- The official language is Central Thai.
- It is a tonal language. The same word may have different meanings depending upon the tone.
- Central Thai is used in the schools. It is also used in government and business.
- There are also regional languages and dialects.
- In some of the northern areas of Thailand, Lao is spoken.
- Along the Cambodian border, Khmer is spoken.
- Chinese and Malay are also used by many people.
- Educated Thais (including people involved in international business) often converse in English.
- Thais in the tourism industry often speak some English (particularly in Bangkok).

Religion

- 95% of the population are Theravada Buddhist.
- 4% of Thais are Muslim.
- 1% practice other religions (including Christianity).
- Buddhism deeply affects the daily lives of the Thai.
- Traditionally, men over the age of 20 are expected to serve as Buddhist monks for at least three months of their lives.
- Although not as prevalent today, this custom is still considered important to the Thai.
- Most Thai faithfully comply to the doctrines of Theravada Buddhism.
- Certain elements of other religions have been incorporated into Buddhism, including ancestor worship, Hinduism, animism, and Brahmanism.

CONDUCTING BUSINESS

Meeting & Greeting

- The traditional and most common greeting in Thailand is called the *wai*.
- Thais will greet foreign business visitors with a handshake. Thais do not expect foreigners to *wai* but are pleased when such courtesy is shown.
- The *wai* movement – which is made by pressing both hands close together in front of one's body, with the fingertips reaching to about neck level – is used to show respect. This is accompanied by a slight bow (women curtsy). The lower the head comes to the hands, the more the respect shown.
- The height and depth of a *wai* denotes social status.
- Unless there is a considerable age difference or social distance between two Thais, it is considered an insult not to return a *wai*.
- The fingertips only go above the level of the eyebrows when revering the Buddha or greeting royalty.
- Fingertips should never go above the head.
- The *wai* can be used to indicate "hello", "good-bye", "thank-you" as well as "I am sorry".
- A *wai* is not used to greet children, servants, street vendors, or laborers.
- If a person is of a lower rank, you should not return a *wai*. The appropriate response is to smile and nod.
- Buddhist monks will never return a *wai*.
- Business cards are important and always exchanged.
- Ideally, cards should have Thai printed on the reverse side.
- Present your card with the Thai side facing the recipient.
- As most Thais are impressed by titles, it is important to have your position or level of authority indicated on your card.
- It is considered impolite to immediately launch into business discussions. Begin the meeting with casual conversation.
- Avoid scheduling trips the week before and after Christmas, as well as during the Chinese and Thai New Year periods. Also avoid the months of April and May (many Thai vacation during this period).

- The best time to schedule a business trip to Thailand is from November to March.
- Allow two to three weeks' notice when scheduling appointments. For an initial meeting, offer several date possibilities.
- English is usually spoken by top management of most companies. If meetings are held outside of Bangkok or with a smaller company, an interpreter may be required.
- Arrange for a letter of introduction. Ideally, have an intermediary.
- Be prepared for the first meeting – especially with government – to end without business being raised; wait for the Thais to take the initiative.
- Try to avoid scheduling appointments very early or very late in the day, particularly in Bangkok. Between 10:00 a.m. and 3:00 p.m. is the best period. When possible, Thais will schedule their arrivals and departures to miss the heaviest part of the morning and evening rush hour traffic.

Forms of Address

- As in the Western tradition, Thai given names come before the family name.
- Address Thais by their given (first) name preceded by their professional (or academic) title, the appropriate English courtesy title (Mr., Mrs, or Miss) or *Khun*.
- As titles are considered very important, use when possible.
- *Khun* is used for men and women, married or single. If you don't know a person's name, you can address them simply as *Khun*.
- Use of surnames is reserved for formal occasions and written communications.
- Last names have only been in use since the 1920's.
- Foreign visitors will be addressed by their first name preceded by Mr., Mrs., or Miss.
- In correspondence, use Dear followed by *Khun* and the given name.
- Nicknames are popular in Thailand. The Thais may give you a nickname, particularly if your name is difficult for them to pronounce.
- Relatives of the royal family occupy many high-level positions. Abbreviations which will indicate a royal connection are the following:
  - P.O.C. – grandchild of a king
  - M.C. – great-grandchild of a king
  - M.R. – great-great-grandchild of a king.
- Many Thai business people are Chinese.
- In Chinese names, the family name is traditionally placed first, followed by the given name.
- Address Chinese using their professional title (Engineer, Dr., President, etc.) or government title (Mayor, Councillor, etc.) followed by their family name.
- If the title is unknown, use the appropriate courtesy title (Mr., Mrs., or Miss) and their family name.
- Never address a Chinese by his or her family name alone.
- Traditionally, Chinese wives retain their maiden name. Marital status is indicated by Madame or Mrs.
- Many Chinese have taken an English first name or use their initials to ease communications with English speakers.
- It is acceptable to ask how someone wishes to be addressed if unsure about which is the family or first name.

ENTERTAINING

- Entertainment is an important part of doing business in Thailand.
- Meals are seen as an opportunity to further develop personal relationships.
- Business entertaining over lunch or dinner is popular. Business breakfasts are not common.
- If scheduling a breakfast, the finer quality hotels are appropriate.
- If entertaining a small group, Western-style hotel restaurants are ideal. For larger gatherings, buffet dinners are appropriate.
- Wait for business discussions to be initiated by your Thai colleagues.
- Business is not usually discussed over lunch.
- The person who has extended the invitation pays for the meal. Never offer to share a bill in a restaurant.
- To attract the attention of a waiter/waitress, extend your hand, palm down, and wave your fingers.
- Do not return a *wai*, if this gesture is initiated by your waiter/waitress. The appropriate response is a smile and a nod.
- Spouses are generally not included in business entertaining.
- After dinner in Bangkok, further evening entertainment usually

includes a visit to a bar in the Patpong Road district. It is impolite to decline.

- Dinner invitations to a private home are rare.
- If entertained in a Thai home, you will often be served dinner buffet-style.
- It is common to be seated on the floor to eat.
- Women should tuck their legs to the side and men sit cross-legged, or with legs tucked to the side (shows special respect to the host).
- Do not stretch out your feet in front of you during a meal.
- Shoes should be removed prior to entering a home.

DINING ETIQUETTE

- The Thai use a fork and spoon. The spoon is held in the right hand and the fork in the left. It is used to push food onto the spoon.
- Knives are usually not necessary because the food is served in small, bite-size portions.
- Chopsticks are used in Chinese restaurants and homes.
- Bones and other food debris should be placed on your plate.
- The standard beverage is water. It is usually consumed at the completion of a meal (rather than during it). As a health precaution, drink water only if it has been poured from a bottle.
- Beer or tea are served and cosumed during the course of the meal.
- Wait for the host to invite you to begin eating.
- Guests are usually served a second helping and are encouraged to eat as much as they can.
- Rice is served. Other dishes are placed in the center of the table. Guests serve themselves; dishes are not passed.
- Do not take the last portion of food from a serving dish. As it is considered an honour to have the last portion of food, wait until it has been offered to you twice. Politely accept on the second offer.
- When finished, place the utensils together on the plate.
- Thai men often smoke following a dinner. Traditional Thai women do not smoke or drink in public. It is acceptable for foreign women to smoke. It is considered polite to offer cigarettes to the men at the dinner. Foreign visitors should wait for smoking to be initiated by the Thai.

PUNCTUALITY

- Although Thais will not always be on time, foreign visitors are expected to be punctual.
- Because of the extremely heavy traffic in Bangkok (it can literally take hours to go across the city in rush hour and during the rainy season), be sure to schedule sufficient time between appointments.

USEFUL PHRASES

Yes
Khrap (said by men)
(krahp)

Yes
Kha (said by women)
(khak)

No
Bplahu krap (said by men)
(blaw krahp)

No
Bplahu ka (said by women)
(blaw kahk)

Please
Garunah
(Ga-roon-nah)

Thank you
Kawp-kun krap (said by men)
(kawp-koon krahp)

Thank you
Kawp-kun ka (said by women)
(kawp-koon kahk)

You're welcome
Mai pen rai krap (said by men)
(my-pen-rye krahp)

You're welcome
Mai pen rai ka (said by women)
(my-pen-rye kahk)

Goodbye (when you are leaving)
Lah gawn krap (said by men)
(law-gahn krahp)

Goodbye (when you are leaving)
Lah gawn ka (said by women)
(law-gahn kahk)

Hello/ Goodbye
Sawat dee khrap (said by men)
(sah-what dee kahp)

Hello/ Goodbye
Sawat dee kha (said by women)
(sah-what dee kahk)

- These expressions can be used either as a general greeting (for any-time during the day) or to say good-bye to someone that is leaving.

VALUES AND SOCIAL CONVENTIONS

- Thailand is a male-dominated society.
- The extended family is the primary social unit. In rural areas, several generations may live together in the same home.
- The monarchy is highly regarded. Proper respect should be shown to anything (money, documents, etc.) that bears a likeness of the king.
- The king is perceived as the symbol of national unity.
- The Thais hold a deep respect for elders and teachers.
- The Thais respect hierarchy and all forms of authority.
- The Thais can be characterized as easy-going, fun-loving, pleasant, patient and hospitable. This is illustrated through their frequent use of words such as *sanuk* (to have fun) and *sabai* (meaning well in the sense of feeling good).
- *Mai pen rai* (never mind) is a popular Thai expression which further characterizes their general approach to life: that it is to be enjoyed. Problems and setbacks should not be taken too seriously.
- Thais are hardworking and generally happy with what they have and who they are.
- Do not speak loudly or show anger in public. You will lose their respect.
- Politeness and maintaining a calm composure are traits that are important to the Thai.
- Most Thai believe in astrologers and will usually consult them about the most auspicious times to begin an important venture.
- Thais believe fate and luck considerably influence their future and the outcome of any venture.
- To bless new buildings or companies, monks and sometimes Brahman priests will be brought in to perform ceremonies - for example in connection with the laying of the foundation.
- Thais will often greet each other with a rhetorical expression "Where are you going" *(Pai nai).* The polite response is "for a walk" (*pai theo* pronounced as pie-tay-oh).
- Thais try to avoid conflict in order to maintain harmony. They will refrain from saying anything negative and are uncomfortable saying an outright "no". "Maybe" or "it might be difficult" generally means "no".
- It is important to be subtle when responding negatively.
- "Yes" does not always means yes. It is necessary to confirm a sense of agreement on things.

BODY LANGUAGE

- Public displays of affection between the sexes is not condoned.
- It is common to see touching between people of the same sex holding hands.
- Women in Thailand – even casual business contacts – will often take a foreign businesswoman's hand when crossing the street.
- Thais smile most of the time. In fact, Thailand has been called "Land of Smiles".
- A smile can mean "hello", "thank you", "yes", "never mind" or excuse me".
- Smiles can also be used to disguise other emotions such as embarrassment.
- Foreign visitors should smile often and in every situation.
- The head should never be touched (even to pat a child's head). The Thai believe it is the most sacred part of the body as it houses the spirit or soul.
- Never pass anything over a person's head.
- Do not pass objects to another person using your left hand.
- The bottoms of your feet are considered the least sacred partof the body and unclean. Never touch anyone, point at anyone, or move objects with your feet.
- Never cross your legs with one leg resting on the other knee.
- Never cross your legs in front of an elderly person or monk.
- Placing an arm over the back of a person's chair while they are sitting is considered offensive.
- Avoid stepping on the doorsill of a wat (Buddhist temple), for the Thais believe that souls reside in doorsills.
- Shoes should be removed before entering a Buddhist temple.
- Do not point using the index finger. Use your hand, palm side up, to point.
- To beckon someone, extend your hand, palm side down, and wave your fingers up and down.
- You should always relinquish your seat on a bus or train to a monk.
- Do not sit next to a monk on a bus, train, or plane.
- Never sit with your head higher than a monk's.
- Women are not permitted to touch a Buddhist monk.
- To receive something from a woman, a monk will extend his robe for the object to be placed on.

CONVERSATION

- The Thais enjoy discussing their cultural heritage.
- Other good topics include: your travels, the beautiful sites of Thailand, Thai cuisine, and Thai classical dance.
- As you get to know them better, talk about your family and enquire about theirs.
- Topics to avoid: the AIDS situation in Thailand, drug trafficking, religion, or regional politics.
- Do not criticize other countries. The Thais may think, "Can someone who criticizes his/her neighbours be trusted?"
- Be sure to avoid any negative reference to Thailand's King and Queen.
- There are strict laws governing the way the Thai may refer to royalty.
- It is illegal for Thais to criticize the monarchy or the government.

TIPPING

- Never leave a one-baht tip. It is considered very insulting.
- Hotels: A 10% to 15% service charge is usually included.
- Restaurants: A 10% service charge is usually included. An extra 10 to 20 baht is appropriate, although not necessary.
- Taxis: A 10% tip. Bargain for a set fare before entering the taxi.
- *Tuk-tuks:* A popular form of transportation. Cheaper than taxis. Agree on a fare before entering.
- Hotel bellmen and room-service waiters: 10 to 50 baht.
- Concierge: 50 to 100 baht.

DRESS & APPEARANCE

- Image and appearance are important to the Thai.
- Dress is seen as a reflection of one's social status.
- Be prepared for high heat and humidity.

Business attire

- Men should wear lightweight suits or trousers and a jacket, white shirt, and tie.
- Women should wear conservative, lightweight tailored suits in any colour (except black, which is associated with mourning), de-emphasizing flashiness except perhaps in evening wear, and low-heeled shoes.

Casual attire

- Men should wear slacks and shirt, with or without ties.
- Women should wear light dresses or skirts and blouses. Avoid sleeveless outfits (they are considered immodest).
- Jeans are acceptable for both sexes.
- Shorts can be worn in public (but not in temples).
- Never wear rubber thong sandals; they are considered very low class.

Evening receptions

- Business attire is usually worn at evening receptions.

Formal events

- Men should wear white jacket, black pants, and black tie.
- Women should wear long dresses.
- Women may wear black at a formal event as long as it is accented by a colour.
- Western-style clothing is very common in Thailand, particularly in the cities.

GIFTS

- Gift giving is less formalized than in the rest of Asia. Gift giving has become quite westernized.
- Gifts are not opened in the presence of the giver.
- Bring a gift for anyone you work with consistently.
- Appropriate business gifts include: illustrated books from your region, special food items, pens, souvenirs from your home country, desk accessories, stationery, brandy/liquor.
- It is customary to bring a small gift when visiting a home.
- Suitable gifts for a hostess include souvenirs from your home country, chocolates, flowers, brandy/liquor, cake or fruit.
- Do not bring carnations or marigolds as they are associated with funerals.
- Gifts should be wrapped in the paper of your choice.

FOR WOMEN

- Foreign businesswomen can succeed in Thailand.
- Although business is dominated by men, increasingly Thai women are entering senior level positions in both business and government.
- Thailand's rapid modernization has also created a class of dynamic, educated, entrepreneurial women who often run their own small-to medium-sized businesses.
- It is acceptable for a foreign businesswoman to invite a Thai businessman to dinner. Do not invite his spouse.

VIETNAM

THE COUNTRY

Population
- 76 million
- More than half are in their teens and early twenties.

Capital
- Hanoi (three million)

Major Cities
- Ho Chi Minh City [formerly Saigon] (5 million)

Government
- Official name of country is the Socialist Republic of Vietnam (since 1976).
- Unicameral National Assembly is the highest governing body.
- Political system dominated by the Vietnamese Communist Party.

Climate
- Basically tropical with relatively high humidity all year. The mountainous interior highlands are cooler.
- In the north, temperatures range from 5C (41F)in the winter or dry season, December to April to 30C (85F) in the summer or wet monsoon season, May through October.
- In the south, temperatures vary only slightly between 25C and 30C (76F and 85F). Rain storms are sudden and torrential.

Electricity
- 220 volts (110 volts in some rural areas)
- Outlets vary requiring a variety of plugs.

Sports
- Volleyball, soccer, badminton, table tennis, and tennis.

Currency
- The *dong* (D)

BUSINESS HOURS

Business Offices
- Monday to Saturday: 8:00 a.m. to 4:30 p.m.
- Close at noon for one hour.

Government Offices
- Monday to Friday: 7:30 a.m. to 4:30 p.m.
- Saturday: 7:30 a.m. to 11:30 a.m. (Posted hours are not always reliable)

Banks
- Monday to Friday: 8:00 a.m. to 4:00 p.m.
- Saturday: 8:00 a.m. to 3:00 p.m.
- Close at 11:00 a.m. on the last working day of each month.
- Break each day between 11:30 a.m. and 1:00 p.m.

Stores
- Monday to Saturday: 8:00 a.m. to 7:00 p.m.
- Most close for two hours at noon.

HOLIDAYS & FESTIVALS

New Year's Day..........January 1
Founding of the Communist Party of Vietnam..........February 3
Vietnamese Lunar New Year (Tet)..........January/February*
Liberation of Saigon/Victory of North Vietnam in 1975..........April 30
Labour Day/International Workers' Day..........May 1
Ho Chi Minh's Birthday..........May 19
Buddha's Birthday (Dan Sinh)..........June*
National Day of the Socialist Republic of Vietnam..........September 2
Christmas..........December 25

*date varies

THE PEOPLE

Ethnic Groups

- 84% Vietnamese
- 2% Chinese
- The rest is comprised of more than 50 different highland minority groups.
- Almost 80% live in rural areas.

Language

- Vietnamese is the official language.
- Many ethnic minorities speak their own native languages at home.
- English, Russian and French are taught in schools. English is the most popular language.
- Older people may speak French.
- Middle-aged Vietnamese may speak Russian.

Religion

- 55% of the population practice Buddhism. Most practice a combination of Buddhism, Taoism, Confucianism, ancestral worship, a little animism, and are superstitious as well.
- 8 to 10% are Roman Catholic.
- .5% practice Islam.
- There are also approximately 2 million followers of Cao Daism, a religion consisting of a blend of religious beliefs plus a reverence of saints. It includes elements from Buddhism, Confucianism, Taoism, Christianity, Islam and ancestral worship. Saints such as Joan of Arc, Victor Hugo, and Napoleon Bonaparte are also revered.
- Hoa Hao has approximately 1.5 million followers. This religion was founded in 1939 by Huynh Phu So . Many of its beliefs are similar to Buddhism.
- Regardless of religious preference, nearly all Vietnamese practice ancestor worship.

CONDUCTING BUSINESS

Meeting & Greeting

- Personal relationships and connections are critical to succeeding in Vietnam.
- If possible, arrange to have important meetings scheduled for the morning as the afternoons are normally reserved for the operational part of the business.
- The exchange of business cards is important. The first card should be given to the most senior person.
- Never write on someone's card.
- The formal greeting is a hand shake followed by a slight nod and bow of the head.
- If the individual is high ranking, use two hands together when shaking hands or exchanging cards.
- The Vietnamese will shake hands with both men and women upon greeting and when saying goodbye.
- Instead of shaking hands, most Vietnamese women will simply bow their head.
- If a hand is not extended, a slight bow of the head is sufficient.
- A formal greeting is *"xin chao"* (seen-chow). Because Vietnamese is a tonal language, many meanings can be indicated, depending upon pronunciation.
- All meetings should begin with casual conversation about the weather, your travels, or events in Vietnam.
- Tea or coffee, along with something to eat, is normally served.
- You should wait until the most senior person has had his first sip before you begin drinking.
- Be sure to taste or drink a small portion of everything offered.
- Business discussions with senior officials should begin a few minutes after light conversation.
- Initial discussions with middle management should focus primarily on relationship building. Wait for your hosts to initiate business discussions.
- If you are using a translator, your attention should always be directed towards the individual you are addressing.

Forms of Address

- The order of a Vietnamese name is family name, middle name, and given name.
- Most Vietnamese use their given names as Westerners would their family names.
- To address a Vietnamese, use his or her given name with the appropriate professional or courtesy title of Mr., Madame, Mrs, Miss, or Dr.
- As a sign of respect, Vietnamese may address a person by their given name plus a title indicating their relationship to one another, as if they were all part of the same family. For example, if a man is greeting a woman of his mother's generation, he may greet her as "aunt" *(co)*.

- Women keep their maiden name after marriage.
- Vietnamese will often address foreigners by their first name and a courtesy title Example: John Smith would be called Mr. John.

ENTERTAINING

- Business lunches and dinners are common.
- When dining out, the person who invites always pays the bill.
- The Vietnamese have a good sense of humour and may entertain you at a speciality restaurant featuring exotic dishes such as snake blood, monkey, or anteater to watch your reaction.
- The Vietnamese will appreciate it if you try any or all of these special delicacies, but will not be offended if you decline. Always indicate your appreciation of the opportunity.
- Never make an impromptu visit to a Vietnamese home. Telephone first or make arrangements to visit at a certain time. Having a foreign guest in one's home is considered an honour. If unprepared, many Vietnamese will feel embarrassed because they are unable to adequately entertain you.
- As a common courtesy, the Vietnamese will automatically serve a drink (and possibly fruit) to a guest, rather than ask first if they would like a drink.
- When visiting a family, if offered food by a Southern Vietnamese, it is impolite to refuse. If you are not hungry, it is important to at least accept a small amount to sit and eat with them.
- In the north, it is the opposite. You should refuse an invitation to eat, unless it is repeated many times.
- In the past, there was very little food and certainly not enough to feed another person. The offer would have been extended as a courtesy, and you would be expected to refuse it.
- If entertained at a home, you should be prepared to make an impromptu thank you speech at some point during the meal.
- If invited to a home, be sure to remove your shoes before entering. Your host will usually provide you with a pair of sandals for indoor use.

DINING ETIQUETTE

- Always hold the rice bowl in your hand. To eat from a rice bowl on the table is considered lazy.
- Never take the last portion of food from a serving dish.
- Always use a serving spoon to take food from a communal dish. Using your chopsticks will "contaminate" the food.
- Be sure to eat all the food in your rice bowl. Leaving anything is considered wasteful and inconsiderate of the efforts required for its preparation.
- Chopsticks should be rested on top of your bowl. It is considered impolite to stick them in the bowl.
- Spoons are provided for soup and should always be held in the left hand.
- It is not considered impolite to make various noises, like slurping, when eating.

PUNCTUALITY

- Punctuality is important to the Vietnamese. Foreign guests should make every effort to be on time. Allowances will be made for situations out of your control i.e. serious traffic congestion.

USEFUL PHRASES

Please
Xin or Xin moi
(seen or seen moy)

Thank you
Cam on
(kahm un)

You're welcome
Khong co chi
(cum gaw chee)

Yes
Ya
(yah)

No
Khong
(cum)

Excuse me
Xin loi
(seen loy)

How are you?
Co manh gioi khong?
(gaw mahn zhoi cum) North
(gas mahn yoi cum) South

VALUES AND SOCIAL CONVENTIONS

- The Vietnamese beliefs and attitudes towards life have been strongly shaped and influenced by religion.
- Maintaining social harmony is extremely important to the Vietnamese.
- Vietnamese have considerable reverance for the elderly and authority.
- Characteristics of the Vietnamese include a deep sense of national pride, resilience, pragmatism, and focused on the future.
- The family is the foundation of Vietnamese society.
- Unlike Western society, aging is not seen in a negative light. The Vietnamese are comfortable with the aging process as their status in society increases.
- The Vietnamese attitude towards happiness is that it is something people are born with, rather than a goal to strive for.
- It is important not to boast or brag about one's achievements, as the Vietnamese believe it is more polite to be self-effacing.
- As with many Asians, Vietnamese are not likely to give a direct "no". They will usually avoid the subject, pretend to misunderstand or answer with a "maybe".
- Avoid public displays of anger. It is considered poor manners.
- Cigarettes will be frequently offered to male visitors. If you don't smoke, avoid showing displeasure. Do not ask your Vietnamese hosts to refrain from smoking in your presence. Foreign women smokers are advised not to smoke unless they wish to attract considerable attention from Vietnamese men.

BODY LANGUAGE

- Do not touch a person's head as it is regarded as the individual's spiritual centre.
- Maintain good posture, as slouching is not looked upon favourably.
- The Vietnamese do not gesture when talking. Avoid excessive hand movements as they will not be understood.
- Men and women do not show affection in public.
- To beckon an individual, extend your hand, palm down, and wiggle all four fingers in unison.
- Do not point at anyone.
- Do not whistle to get someone's attention.
- Showing the sole of your foot is considered rude. It is therefore best to avoid crossing your legs at meetings.
- It is common for people of the same sex to hold hands while walking. It is a sign of friendship.
- Don't be surprised if your business associate tries to hold your hand while walking, as it simply indicates that they are comfortable with you.
- Both hands should be used when passing something to another person.
- It is considered impolite to cross the index and middle fingers.

CONVERSATION

- In business, polite conversation will include discussions about families, where you are from, your travels, and how you have enjoyed your stay.
- In more established relationships, it is considered polite to inquire about the health of family members.

TIPPING

- Restaurants: If there is no service charge, it is customary to leave a tip of 10% of the bill.
- Hotels: A service charge is normally included in the bill.
- Taxis: No tips are necessary, unless the trip is late at night.
- Bell boys: US $1
- Maids: US $1
- Toilet Attendants: Small change

DRESS & APPEARANCE

- For business, men should wear conservative, lightweight suits and ties. Women should wear a conservative dress, suit, or slacks with a blouse.
- Vietnamese business women seldom dress formally in Western-style suits. Often they will wear the traditional ao dai, or may prefer a simple skirt and blouse.
- For casual attire, slacks and a cotton shirt are appropriate for both men and women.
- Shorts should only be worn at the beach.

GIFTS

- Gifts are often given at the end of meetings or upon the completion of a transaction.
- Always bring a small gift for the hostess, or the children, if you are invited to a Vietnamese home.
- If invited to a home, do not bring food items as this may be seen as an insult by your host.
- Gifts should always be nicely wrapped in colourful paper.
- Gifts will not be opened in the presence of the giver.
- Colours and animals have symbolic meanings. Good colours include: red, purple, green, and blue. Colours to avoid include: black and white (although there are some exceptions with white as it can symbolize purity. For example, young women wear white *ao dais.* This is the flattering traditional dress for women which consists of long, wide-legged pants worn under a high-necked long-sleeved dress).
- Animals with a positive connotation include: turtles (endurance); dragons (good luck); cranes (longevity); and spiders (money). Those with a negative connotation include: cows (stupid); pigs (lazy and stupid); monkeys (bad), and ravens or owls (death).
- Do not give handkerchiefs. During the war, young girls gave handkerchiefs, which had their name embroidered on the corner, to their boyfriends who were going off to war. Many men did not return and the handkerchiefs are now often associated with grief and parting.
- Knives symbolize fighting.
- Gifts of perfume may suggest that you think the person smells.
- Popular gifts include: expensive chocolates, imported foods, ties, quality pens, shirts, whisky, cognac or gifts from your home country.

FOR WOMEN

- Women should dress conservatively. Avoid heavy make-up or revealing clothing or you may be viewed as a prostitute.
- Little sexual discrimination exists in Vietnam.
- It is not a difficult place for a foreign woman to conduct business.
- Women should avoid smoking or drinking in public. Both will reduce their chances of being taken seriously.
- If entertaining a Vietnamese man, a woman should insist on paying for the meal.
- If entertained by a Vietnamese man, a woman should always reciprocate with a meal of equal value.

APPENDIX: MAJOR ASIAN RELIGIONS

To understand Asian cultures, it is necessary to have at least a passing familiarity with the basic tenets of their religions, as they are the cornerstone of Asian beliefs, values, and even daily activities.

The following is a brief overview of the major religions mentioned in this book. The summary offered is intended to be only an introduction to these faiths. The reader may wish to supplement this reference by reading additional sources.

ANCESTOR WORSHIP

- Ancestor worship is not considered a religion on its own. It is always part of a larger religious system.
- Ancestor worship has been incorporated into many religions throughout the world (although there will be variations on the practice according to country and religion).
- Ancestor worship plays an important role in the religious systems of Korea, China, Japan and Taiwan.
- The beliefs and customs focus on the veneration and worship of deceased family members.
- The premise is that deceased ancestors can influence the lives of living descendants.
- Depending upon the culture, ancestors can have the characteristics of being: a) both supportive as well as punishing, or b) exclusively helpful or c) strictly punishing.
- Rituals and ceremonies are conducted to keep the spirits happy so that wealth and good fortune will result.
- Private worship is done with ancestor tablets in the home. These tablets contain the names of deceased ancestors over several generations.
- Most public worship takes place in an edifice that has been built exclusively for this purpose.

ANIMISM

- Animism is usually combined with other beliefs such as magic, witchcraft or shamanism to form a religion.
- Animism occurs in approximately 50% of the world's cultures.
- Animism is based upon the premise that an animal, plant or object is imbued with a spirit or soul which can influence human life in a negative or positive way.
- The belief is that these spirits can be influenced and are responsive to prayer, offerings, and adherence to rituals

BUDDHISM

History

- Buddhism is based upon the life and teachings of Siddhartha Gautama (later known as Buddha), a prince who lived in the sixth and fifth centuries B.C. in what is now Nepal.
- The word Buddha comes from the Sanskrit root budh which means both to

wake up and to know. Buddha therefore means the *"Enlightened one"* or *"Awakened One"*.

- Buddhism evolved as a widespread reaction against Hinduism in India.
- Siddhartha abandoned his life of privilege and wealth at the age of 29 after witnessing four events that changed his life: a frail old man, a sick suffering old man, a corpse, and an ascetic monk.
- Siddartha left his home in search of the solution for human suffering.
- Siddhartha led the life of an ascetic for six years, seeking the wisdom of two Hindu gurus and eventually joining up with five other ascetics.
- Siddhartha subjected himself to extreme self-abuse and outdid his associates in every austerity they proposed (which almost led to his death).
- This experience taught him the futility of austerity and thus he rejected it as the path to enlightenment.
- In frustration, Siddhartha found a large sheltering tree, known as the Bodhi tree, and decided to remain in meditation there until an answer to his quandary could be found.
- Siddhartha's enlightenment was said to have occurred at this point.
- Armed with this new knowledge, Siddhartha became the Buddha.
- Although Buddhism teaches tolerance of other religions, Buddhists have been historically subjected to persecution.
- There are very few Buddhists left in India (where the religion originated) because of actions taken by Hindu leaders in the 13th century.

Beliefs

- Central to Buddha's teachings are the four Noble Truths:
  1. Life is inherently imperfect, full of sorrow and suffering
  2. Desire is the cause of this suffering
  3. Suffering can cease by eliminating earthly desires
  4. The path is the Middle Way (which avoids both extreme self-denial and unrestrained self-indulgence) and the Noble Eightfold Path.
- The Noble Eightfold Path consists of the following:
  1. Right Views (person believes in the four noble truths)
  2. Right Intention (to resist evil).
  3. Right Speech (saying nothing to hurt others)
  4. Right Conduct (respecting others)
  5. Right Occupation (working at a job that does not violate the above prohibitions)
  6. Right Effort (attempting to stay away from evil)
  7. Right Contemplation (controlling thoughts and emotions)
  8. Right Concentration (meditation)

- The ultimate goal is to reach *nirvana* or state of perfect peace and happiness.
- There is no central god figure in Buddhism.
- Buddhists believe spiritual enlightenment can be found within all people.
- Today there are two major schools of Buddhism, Hinayana (or Theravada) and Mahayana.

Theravada Buddhism

- Theravada Buddhism is a more conservative or orthodox interpretation of Buddha's teachings.
- The Theravada school believes that Siddhartha was the great teacher and the only enlightened one, but that he was not divine.
- The Theravada believe only ordained monks and nuns can achieve nirvana.

Mahayana Buddhism

- Mahayana is a more liberal interpretation.
- The Mahayana Buddhists regard Buddha as a living incarnation of the Buddha spirit. Siddhartha was only one of many mortal "enlightened ones".
- The Mahayana believe that anyone can achieve nirvana

Zen Buddhism

- Zen is a sect of Mahayana Buddhism which exists in Japan.
- Silent meditation is practiced in order to achieve serenity of the mind and the higher state of being.

CONFUCIANISM

- Confucianism is named after Confucius.
- Confucius was born in northern China in 551 B.C. and died in 479 B.C.
- Experts disagree as to whether Confucianism is a religion or a philosophy.
- A god, or gods, are not worshipped.
- Some features of Confucianism that are common to religion include a belief in heaven, ancestor worship, rituals, and sacrifices.
- Confucianism has played a major role in Chinese social, political, and religious life for over 2,000 years.
- Confucianism has also had a tremendous influence in Vietnam, Korea, and Japan.
- Confucius is believed to be the first person in China to develop a code of ethics.
- Confucianism preaches a strong work ethic, education, ancestor worship and obligations to family, society and the state.

HINDUISM

History

- The word Hindu is derived from the Persian word *Hind.*
- *Hind* relates to the region around the Indus River in northern India.
- Around 1500 B.C., Aryan invaders (from central Asia) settled in India.
- This group ultimately dominated India

and set into practice their religious beliefs and customs, including the caste system of social organization.

- More than 98% of Hindus live in India.
- Hinduism does not have a human founder.
- Hinduism is a collection of many related religious beliefs and practices.
- There are believed to be more than one million gods in Hinduism.
- There are several ancient Hindu texts that describe the philosphies of this faith.
- The most important texts include the *Vedas*, the *Brahmanas*, the *Upanishads*, and the *Aranyakas.*
- The *Vedas*, the oldest of Hindu sacred writings, include about one thousand hymns to different gods, chants, sacrificial rituals, magical spells, incantations and other ritualistic practices.
- The *Brahmanas* were written after the *Vedas.* These writings describe ritual practices and the mystical meanings of various rites.
- The *Upanishads* offer the basic philosophy behind Hinduism.
- The *Aranyakas* offer esoteric descriptions of humanity and the world.
- There are also numerous epic stories about gods, heroes, and saints.
- The epics include the *Ramayana* and the *Mahabharata.*

Beliefs

- The underlying premise of Hinduism is the concept of reincarnation. This is the belief that humans will go through a perpetual series of rebirths in which a soul takes on any form of life (animal, vegetable, or human).
- An individual's form of rebirth will be determined by his or her *Karma.*
- *Karma* is a result of a person's thoughts and actions. This will dictate what form that person will assume in his or her next life.
- This continuous chain can only end once a person has reached spiritual perfection.

Caste System

- One of the most distinctive characteristics of Hinduism is the caste system.
- The caste system is very complex and defines a social order.
- It was originally developed by the Brahmins (priests) to ensure their superior position was permanent.
- The five main social categories are: Brahmins (priests), Kshatriyas (rulers and warriors), Vaisya (farmers, and merchants), Sudra (labourers and craftsmen), and the "Untouchables" (who perform the most menial and degrading jobs).
- The Untouchables are considered so low in status as to be outside of the caste system.

APPENDIX: MAJOR ASIAN RELIGIONS

ISLAM

- Islam is the second largest religion in the world (Christianity is the first).
- The followers of Islam are called Muslims.
- "Islam" means "submission" (submission to the will of God [Allah]).
- "Muslim" means "he who submits".
- Islam was founded in A.D. 662 by the Arab prophet Muhammed.

History

- Muhammed was born in about A.D. 570 in Mecca.
- He was a merchant and husband until the year 610 when God revealed himself.
- He left Mecca in 622. This is known as Hijra (the year of emigration) and marks the first year in the Muslim calendar.
- He settled in Yathrib (known as the City of the Prophet or Medina).

Beliefs

- The religion of Islam recognizes the previous prophets or messengers of God, including Adam, Abraham, Moses, Ishamel, and Jesus Christ.
- Muhammed is considered to be the last prophet of God.
- The book of holy scripture is called the Koran (also spelled Qur'an).
- The Koran is considered to be the written version of the will of Allah as described to Muhammed.
- The Koran outlines strict rules of social behaviour.
- Islam believes there is a heaven (Paradise) and a hell.
- To enter Paradise, a Muslim has five fundamental obligations. These duties are known as the Five Pillars of Islam.

The Five Pillars of Islam are as follows:

1. Allegiance to Islam.
2. Pray five times daily.
3. Voluntary contribution of money for the poor.
4. Make a least one pilgrimage, or haj, in a lifetime to Mecca if health and circumstances allow.
5. Fast during the month of Ramadan to demonstrate one's faith through personal sacrifice.

SHINTO

- Shinto, which literally means "the way of the gods/spirits", is the indigenous religion of Japan.
- Shinto is a collective term covering the hundreds of religious customs used in the worship of *kami.*
- *Kami* is the spiritual force or godlike essence that exists in all forms of nature, including mountains, rivers, rocks and trees.
- The date of its origin is unknown.
- In the fifth and sixth centuries Shinto was heavily influenced by Confucianism.

- Shinto emphasizes rituals and moral standards.
- The blessings of gods must be obtained for daily events (such as weddings, births, and the establishment of new companies).
- Shintoism is tolerant of other religions.
- Buddhism was integrated with Shintoism, to the degree that Buddhist temples were built under the direction of Shinto priests.
- Shintoism focuses on maintaining ritual purity and a high respect for nature.

TAOISM

- Taoism, meaning "the way", is one of the two religious philosophies, along with Confucianism, that has shaped Chinese life for the last 2,000 years.
- Taoism (also spelled Daoism) arose from the philosphy of Lao Tzu (Laotse), who was born in China around 604 B.C.
- Taoism is practiced in China, Korea, Malaysia, the Philippines, Singapore, Taiwan and Vietnam.
- The founding document is the *Tao Te Ching* (The Way and Its Power), which traditionalists say was written by Lao Tzu. It is believed to have been written between the sixth and fourth centuries B.C.
- The text lays out the five fundamental principles of Taoism: Tao, relativity, nonaction, return and government.

Beliefs

- Taoism revolves around the concept of Tao (literally means "path" or "way").
- This Tao cannot be perceived or even clearly conceived, for it is too vast for human rationality to fathom.
- Tao is understood as emptiness and the basis of all being.
- Taoism is tied in with the traditional Chinese *yin/yang* symbol. This polarity sums up all of life's basic oppositions: good/evil, active/passive, positive/negative, light/dark, summer/winter, and male/female.
- Although in this symbol the halves are in tension, they are not flatly opposed; they complement and balance each other. Each half invades the other's hemisphere. In the end, both find themselves resolved by the circle that surrounds them, the Tao in its eternal wholeness.
- The object of Taoism is to align one's daily life to the Tao.
- Selflessness, cleanliness, and emotional calm are the preliminaries to arriving at full self-knowledge, but they must include deep meditation.
- The Taoists reject all forms of self-assertiveness and competition. Humility is revered.

SOURCES & REFERENCES

Acuff, Frank L. *How to negotiate anything with anyone anywhere around the world.* New York: AMACOM, 1993.

Axtell, Roger E., ed. *Do's and Taboos Around the World.* 2nd edition. New York: John Wiley & Sons, 1991.

Axtell, Roger E. *Do's and Taboos of Hosting International Visitors.* New York: John Wiley & Sons, 1990.

Axtell, Roger E. Gestures. *The Do's and Taboos of Body Language Around the World.* New York: John Wiley & Sons, 1991.

Axtell, Roger E., Tami Briggs, Margaret Corcoran, and Mary Beth Lamb. *Do's and Taboos Around the World for Women in Business.* New York: John Wiley & Sons, 1997.

Bardaman, James M., Jr. and Michiko Sasaki Vardaman. *Japanese Etiquette Today.* Charles E. Tuttle Company, 1994.

Bosrock, Mary Murray. *Put Your Best Foot Forward (Asia).* International Education Systems, 1994.

Brake, Terence, Danielle Medina Walker, and Thomas D. Walker. *Doing Business Internationally: The Guide to Cross-Cultural Success.* Burr Ridge, IL: Irwin Professional Publishing, 1994.

Branne, Christalyn & Tracey Wilen. *Doing Business With Japanese Men.* Stone Bridge Press, 1993.

Brooks, Guy & Victoria. *Indonesia, A kick start guide for business travelers.* International Self-Counsel Press Ltd., 1995.

Brooks, Guy & Victoria. *Malaysia, A kick start guide for business travelers.* International Self-Counsel Press Ltd., 1995.

Brooks, Guy & Victoria. *Vietnam, A kick start guide for business travelers.* International Self-Counsel Press Ltd., 1995.

SOURCES & REFERENCES

Canadian Women doing business in Asia. Industry, Science & Technology Canada and Asia Pacific Foundation of Canada, 1992.

Chambers, Kevin. *The Travelers' Guide to Asian Customs and Manners.* New York: Meadowbrook, 1998.

Collins, Robert J. *Japan-Think, Ameri-Think.* Penguin Books, 1992.

Collins, Terah Kathryn. *The Western Guide to Feng Shui.* Hay House, Inc. 1996.

Condon, John C. *With Respect to the Japanese.* Intercultural Press Inc., 1984.

Copeland, Lennie and Lewis Griggs. *Going International: How to Make Friends and Deal Effectively in the International Marketplace.* New York: Random House, 1985.

Craig, JoAnn Meriwether. *Culture Shock, Singapore.* Graphic Arts Center Publishing, 1997.

Crystal, David (editor). *The Cambridge Factfinder (3rd ed.).* Cambridge University Press, 1998.

Curry, Jeffrey and "Jim" Chinh Nguyen. *Passport Vietnam.* World Trade Press, 1997.

DeMente, Boye Lafayette. *Japanese Etiquette & Ethics in Business.* NTC Business Books, 1995.

Draine, Cathie and Barbara Hall. *Culture Shock, Indonesia.* Graphic Arts Center Publishing, 1997.

Dunung, Sanjyot P. *Doing Business in Asia.* Lexington Books, 1995.

Ellis, Claire. *Culture Shock, Vietnam.* Graphic Arts Center Publishing Company. 1997.

SOURCES & REFERENCES

Engholm, Christopher. *When Business East Meets Business West.* New York: John Wiley & Sons.

Ferraro, Gary P. *The Cultural Dimension of International Business.* Prentice Hall, 1998.

Gombrich, Richard. *Theravada Buddhism.* Routledge, 1995.

Hope, Jane and Borin Van Loon. *Buddha for Beginners.* Icon Books Ltd. 1995.

Hoskin, John. *Thailand, The Kingdom of Siam.* Passport Books, 1988.

Hur, Sonja Vegdahl. Culture Shock, Korea. Graphic Arts Center Publishing Company, 1997.

Kolanad, Gitanjali. *Culture Shock, India.* Graphic Arts Center Publishing Company, 1997.

James, David L. *The Executive Guide to Asia-Pacific Communications.* Kodansha International, 1995.

Leaptrott, Nan. *Rules of the Game: Global Business Protocol.* Thomas Executive Press, 1996.

Mansfield, Stephen. *Culture Shock, Laos.* Graphic Arts Center Publishing Company, 1998

Mittmann, Karin and Zafar Ihsan. *Culture Shock, Pakistan.* Graphic Arts Center Publishing Company, 1996.

Morrison, Terri, Wayne A. Conaway, and George A. Borden, PhD. *Kiss, Bow, or Shake Hands.* Bob Adams, Inc., 1994.

Nelson, Carl A. *Protocol for Profit.* International Business Press, 1998.

Ricks, David A. *Blunders in International Business.* Blackwell Publishers, 1997.

Rossman, Marlene L. *The International Businesswoman of the 1990s.* New York: Praeger, 1986.

Samovar, Larry A., Richard E. Porter and Lisa A. Stefani. *Communication Between Cultures.* Wadsworth Publishing Company, 1998.

Shanson, T.L. *International Guide to Forms of Address.* MacMillian Publishers, 1997.

Sharp, Ilsa. *Culture Shock, Australia.* Times Book International. 1992.

Sinclair, Kevin with Irish Wong Po-yee. *Culture Shock - China.* Graphic Arts Center Publishing Company, 1997.

Skabelund, Grant Paul (managing ed.). *Culturgrams.* Provo, UT: Brigham Young University, David M. Kennedy Center for International Studies, 1993.

Snowden, Barbara. *The Global Edge: How Your Company Can Win in the International Marketplace.* New York: Simon & Schuster, 1986.

Storey, Robert. *Taiwan, A Travel Survival Kit.* Lonely Planet, 1987.

The World Alamanac and Book of Facts 1999. World Almanac Books, 1998.

Training Management Corporation. *Doing Business Internationally.* Princeton Training Press, 1997.

Wei, Betty and Elizabeth Li. *Culture Shock, Hong Kong.* Graphic Arts Publishing Company, 1995.

White, Gayle Colquitt. *Believers and Beliefs.* Berkley Books, 1997.

Wilen, Tracey and Patricia Wilen. *Asia for Women on Business.* Stone Bridge Press, 1995.

Wise, Naomi. *Passport Thailand.* World Trade Press, 1997.

Wong, Jan. *Red China Blues.* Double Day/Anchor Books, 1997.

INDEX

INDEX

CANADIAN ORDER FORM

Fax Orders: 416-441-6801

Telephone Orders: 416-441-3519
or 1-888-347-1116

Postal Orders: Trade Winds Publications,
740 York Mills Rd,
Suite 201, Toronto,
Ontario, Canada
M3B 1W7

TRADE WINDS
COMMUNICATIONS

Please send me ☐ copies of ***Raise Your Cultural IQ***

Company:______________________________

Name:______________________________

Address:______________________________

City:______________________________

Provincc:______________________________

Telephone Number: (___)__________________________

Price per Book CDN $17.95 plus G.S.T.

(Single copy price $22.50 including G.S.T. & shipping and handling – regular mail)

INQUIRE ABOUT VOLUME DISCOUNTS

Payment:

- ❏ Cheque (Please make payable to Trade Winds Publications Inc.)
- ❏ Credit Card (VISA only)

  Card Number ________________________

  Name on Card ________________________

  Expiry Date ________________________

CALL TOLL FREE 1-888-347-1116

INTERNATIONAL ORDER FORM

Fax Orders: 416-441-6801

Telephone Orders: 416-441-3519
or 1-888-347-1116

Postal Orders: Trade Winds Publications,
740 York Mills Rd,
Suite 201, Toronto,
Ontario, Canada
M3B 1W7

TRADE WINDS
COMMUNICATIONS

Please send me ☐ copies of ***Raise Your Cultural IQ***

Company:______________________________

Name:______________________________

Address:______________________________

City:______________________________

Province:______________________________

Telephone Number: (___)______________________________

Price per Book U.S. $11.95 plus shipping
(Single copy price $15.95 including shipping & handling – regular mail)

INQUIRE ABOUT VOLUME DISCOUNTS

Payment:

❑ Cheque (Please make payable to Trade Winds Publications Inc.)
❑ Credit Card (VISA only)

Card Number ______________________________

Name on Card ______________________________

Expiry Date ______________________________

CALL TOLL FREE 1-888-347-1116

To arrange author interviews, special events, or lectures please contact:

Trade Winds Communications

740 York Mills Road, Suite 201

Toronto, Ontario M3B 1W7

Canada

Telephone: (1 416) 441-3519

Fax: (1 416) 441-6801

Email: twind@inforamp.net

Web: www.tradewindscom.com